# KIDS
## AND
# GRANDPARENTS
## AN ACTIVITY BOOK

WRITTEN BY ANN LOVE & JANE DRAKE
ILLUSTRATED BY HEATHER COLLINS

KIDS CAN PRESS

First U.S. edition 2000

Text © 1999 Ann Love and Jane Drake
Illustrations © 1999 Heather Collins

Kids Can Press acknowledges the support of the Ontario Arts Council, the Canada Council for the Arts and the Government of Canada, through the BPIDP, for our publishing activity.

Published in Canada by
Kids Can Press Ltd.
29 Birch Avenue
Toronto, ON M4V 1E2

Published in the U.S. by
Kids Can Press
2250 Military Road
Tonawanda, NY 14150

www.kidscanpress.com

Edited by Laurie Wark
Designed by Blair Kerrigan/Glyphics

Printed and bound in Hong Kong by Book Art Inc., Toronto

CM 99 0 9 8 7 6 5 4 3 2
CM PA 99 0 9 8 7 6 5 4 3 2

Canadian Cataloguing in Publication Data

Love, Ann
    Kids and Grandparents: An Activity Book

ISBN 1-55074-784-3 (bound)   ISBN 1-55074-492-5 (pbk.)

1. Amusements. 2. Grandparent and child. I. Drake, Jane. II. Collins, Heather. III. Title.

GV1229.L68 1999        790.1'922        C99-931918-3

Kids Can Press is a Nelvana company

## ACKNOWLEDGMENTS

Doreen Barnett; Barbara and Victor Barnett; Fran and Will Barnett; Joyce Barnett; Judy and Ian Barnett; June Barrett; Betsy Bascom; Fran and David Bean; Neil Beatty; Julie Booker; Ruth and Jack Brickenden; Trish Brooks; Jennifer Cayley; Kay and Arthur Cayley; Karen Hilbourn Chaplin; Becky Cheung; Nicky and Paul Chumas; Kath Clay; Linda Clark; Jane Morley Cobden; Wendy Cox; Jane Crist; Alan Downward; Gerri, Jane and Paula Draimin; Cindy and Tom Drake; Jim, Stephanie, Brian and Madeline Drake; Dressmaker's Supply; Mary Dobson; Maria Ennes; Muriel and Ellsworth Flavelle; Jayne Frye; Angela Gallo; Tom and Carol Gourlay; Judy Green; Eve Gruss; Kate and Will Halliday; Margie Stockwell Hart; Tom and Sally Hawks; Ann McDonald Hilmer; Elizabeth Hoey; Ken Hook; Willo Horsfall; Heather Irwin; Helen Jones; Martha Kilgour; Marion Knisley; Bob and Judy Lank; Jackie Leech; Kathleen and Donald Leitch; David, Melanie, Jennifer and Adrian Love; Peter Love; Charmian and Frank Manchee; Wendy Corrigan McCreath; Kit and Murray McDonald; Betty MacPherson; Grace Mitchell; David and Roz Morley; Sharon Moss; Donna O'Connor; Diane Peck; Michael Perley; Annette Portello; Maria Price; Wendy Reifel; Hilary Robinson; Michael Roth; Sukhi Sandhu; Jack and Yvonne Sellers; Elsie Simpson; Stephanie Smith; Marjory and John Snowden; Barb and Jack Spitler; Doug and Jane Stewart; Ruth and Walt Stewart; Marcia Syer; Doris Tanter; Bob and Kay Taylor; Mary Thompson; Derek Totten; Deb Dewar Wells; Madeline Woolatt; Elizabeth Vosburgh

Thank you to Valerie Hussey, Ricky Englander and all the people at Kids Can Press. As we've come to expect, illustrator Heather Collins and designer Blair Kerrigan have helped to bring this book to life. Thanks to you both. Special thanks to our editor, Laurie Wark, who had a vested interest in this project. We hope her two young boys will use it with their grandparents!

**W**ith memories of Grandma, Grandpa, Momma and Poppa and with thanks to Granny Kay and Boey, Grandma Ruthie and Grandpa Charlie, Granny and Charles

# CONTENTS

# INTRODUCTION

**Y**ou may have one grandparent, two, or even four. In any case, you're lucky — grandparents are special friends. As you spend time with your grandparents, you will talk, laugh and swap stories. This book is packed with questions and activities that will help you discover the craziest and happiest family stories of all.

Take this book when you visit your grandparents. And have it handy when a grandparent comes to your place. You'll find activities you can do only with a grandparent — like drawing a family tree, designing a family crest or learning a family tale. Discover games and crafts your grandparents did as kids. Have fun with your grandparents and find out lots about yourself and your family at the same time.

# MAKING MEMORIES

**Y**our grandparents can tell you the true-life adventures of your ancestors. Together you can share your family story in many ways.

Track your forebears' travels on a
map, draw an ancestral tree, sew
a family quilt,
make a family crossword puzzle
and

much more.
This chapter
shows you how
to collect old memories
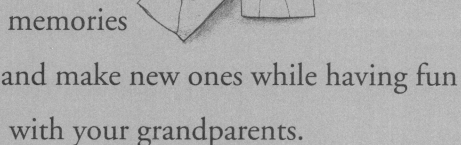 and make new ones while having fun
 with your grandparents.

# MEMORY BOOK

**C**an you remember everything you've done with your grandparents in the last year — skating at New Year's? a week at the trailer park during Spring Break? Create a personalized memory book to record all the great things you do together. Glue in mementos: greeting cards, photographs, programs, entrance tickets and score sheets. Add notes about those special times together.

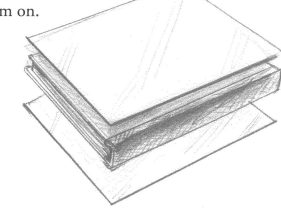

### YOU'LL NEED

a large scrapbook

duct tape

heavy cardboard

a glue stick

scissors

a ruler

a pencil

markers, paints, stickers or other decorating supplies

**1.** Reinforce the spine of the book with duct tape.

**2.** Measure and cut two pieces of cardboard to fit the covers, leaving the spine of the book free to move. Glue them on.

## MEMORY BOX

**I**f you'd rather keep your memories together in a box, try making a shoebox collage. Glue a sampling of keepsakes to the outside of a shoebox, overlapping them so the entire box is covered. Using a paintbrush, seal the collage with a thin coating of white glue. The glue will dry clear. When dry, fill the box with your other mementos. Make one for your grandparents as a thank-you or birthday gift.

**3.** Decorate the cover and add a title and the date.

**4.** Keep photos, postcards, letters, ticket stubs and anything else that links you to your grandparents. Paste the items into your book. Add new mementos as you receive them and remember to date each entry.

# FAMILY TREE

**W**here did your family come from? Who are you related to? Have you any interesting ancestors you haven't heard about? To answer these questions, become the family genealogist (someone who studies ancestors). Begin by interviewing a grandparent. Set aside quiet time together, and ask questions.

**1.** Find out the full names, birthdays and birthplaces of parents, uncles, aunts, cousins, grandparents and their parents.

**2.** Note interesting information, such as Great Aunt Susan had curly red hair or Cousin Cecil went to jail for forgery.

**3.** In the case of dead relatives, record when and where they died.

After the interview, there will be gaps in your family history such as forgotten names and dates. Ask your grandparents if they have any of the documents listed here and search through them for missing information. Together you may complete the puzzle of your family tree. Then, see page 14 to make a pedigree chart.

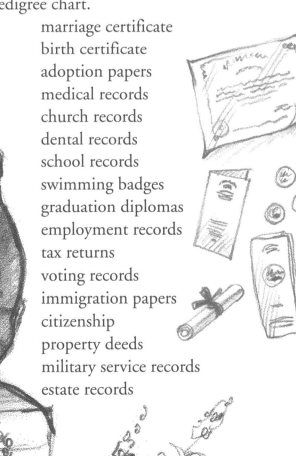

marriage certificate
birth certificate
adoption papers
medical records
church records
dental records
school records
swimming badges
graduation diplomas
employment records
tax returns
voting records
immigration papers
citizenship
property deeds
military service records
estate records

## ARE WE RELATED?

If you can't figure out how someone is related to you, check this list. Whether it's through bloodlines, common law or marriage, all relatives and relationships belong on your pedigree chart.

**great grandparent** – the parent of a person's grandparent

**first cousin** – the child of a person's uncle or aunt

**first cousin once removed** – the child of a first cousin

**second cousins** – what children of first cousins call each other

**third cousins** – what the children of second cousins call each other

**second cousin once removed** – the child of a second cousin

**stepfather or stepmother** – a parent's new spouse

**stepbrothers and stepsisters** – children of a stepparent

**half brothers and half sisters** – children who share only one biological parent

**adoptive parent** – parent of a child who has been legally adopted

## GLOSSARY OF GENEALOGICAL TERMS

**ancestor** – a relative from long ago

**biological relative** – someone related by blood such as mother, father or sister

**common law** – a marriage that is recognized by common law

**descendant** – a person whose lineage can be traced to a family

**in-laws** – relatives by marriage

**kin** – family or relatives

**lineage** – a person's direct line to his or her ancestors

**sibling** – a brother or a sister

# PEDIGREE CHART

A pedigree chart brings your family history to life. Fill in the blanks, adding any interesting facts you uncover. You may find out where you got your crooked smile or your artistic talent.

### YOU'LL NEED

4 to 6 large sheets of plain white paper

a ruler

a fine-tipped black marker

**1.** Copy this chart onto the paper. You are number 1. Fill in the details of when and where you were born.

**2.** Use all the information gathered from your family and fill in the other numbers.

**3.** Your parents are numbers 2 and 3. Your father's parents are 4 and 5, your mother's parents are 6 and 7, and so on.

**4.** The skeleton's closet is reserved for an ancestor you think was wild and exciting.

**5.** When your research is finished, make a good copy for your grandparents. Add to it as people join or leave your family.

## DIGGING DEEPER

If you want to explore your family tree right down to its roots, ask librarians for help. They can show you books and microfiche as well as assist with CD ROM and Internet searches. Depending on where your relatives came from, it may be possible to trace back a long way. India has records for more than 1000 years, Europe 1700 years and the Middle East 1300 years. Who knows, you may discover that you're related to someone famous, or to a terrible scoundrel!

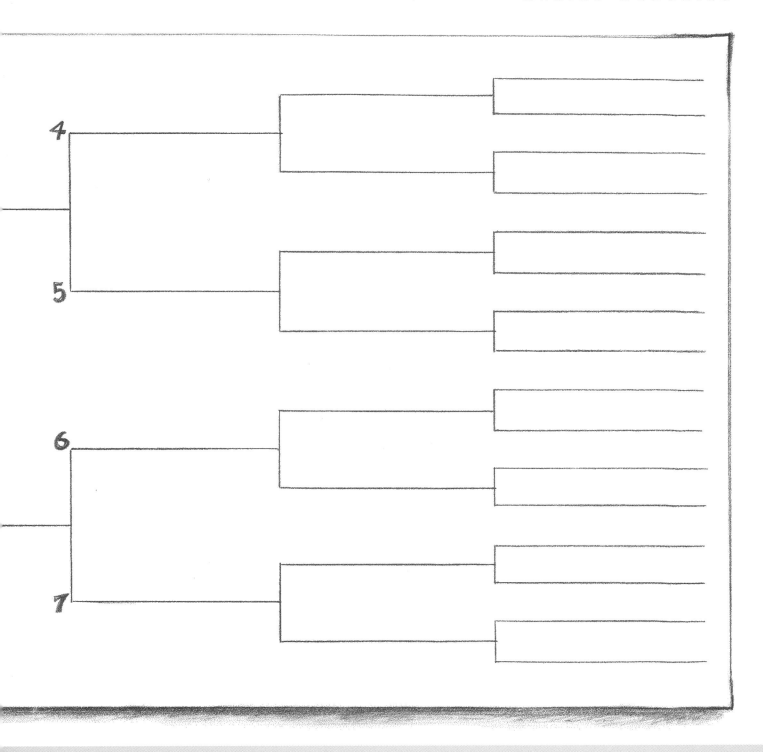

4

5

6

7

## DOG PEDIGREE

**P**urebred dogs have pedigree charts too. Each pup has a litter number, name and birthday as well as the names of her parents. A dog's fur, how she stands, holds her tail and the length of her snout all show her bloodlines.

15

# RELATIVE MAP

**W**hy do you live where you do? You can start answering that question if you track the travels of past family members on a map. In the process, you'll probably discover some wonderful family stories.

## YOU'LL NEED

a world map

sticky notes

a pencil

markers in different colors

Great-great-great grandfather James Gourlay, born 1855 watchmaker in Detroit (father of 7 children)

Great-great-great-great grandfather Harry Gourlay, born County Fermanagh, Ireland 1830, 8th of 11 children sailed to America, settled in upper New York State.

Great-great grandmother Ellen Gourlay, born 1878 a schoolteacher, worked in Klondike, then Vancouver, Canada, married Ivan Jurkus, violinist and prospector.

Great-great uncle Thomas Jurkus, born 1898 in Vancouver killed in Italy World War II

Dad (born 1959) and Mom (born 1961) honeymooned in Hawaii, live in Seattle.

Grandmother Ruth Jurkus, born 1939 in Seattle nurse in Lima married Joseph Gallo, biologist, currently lives in California

**1.** Check your family tree (see page 12) for the name of your oldest-known ancestor and when and where that person was born.

**2.** Locate that birthplace on the map and mark it with a sticky note. Write down the person's name, approximate birth date and relationship to you. Ask your grandparents for any other important details about your ancestor's life, such as occupation, and add them to the note.

**3.** Continue to name and locate your forebears down to the present. When a family member traveled somewhere, place a sticky note at the destination and draw a pencil line along the route. Indicate whether the relative settled there, moved on or returned home.

**4.** When you know your information is correct, go over the travel lines with a marker.

# FAMILY CREST

**S**ome families have crests that show their strengths, deeds or beliefs. Ancient family crests are found carved on walls, furniture, jewelry or ornaments. Once you know some family history, you can design a crest to represent your family. If you find that your family has always loved sports, enjoyed playing the fiddle and had dogs as pets, your crest could have a dog sitting on a baseball glove with a violin in one paw and a bow in the other.

### YOU'LL NEED

a rolling pin

self-hardening clay or baking clay (see page 156)

a cookie sheet

a knife

a fork

tempera paints and a paint brush

materials for decoration such as buttons, beads, feathers, yarn

## CRESTS AND COATS OF ARMS

**A** thousand years ago in Europe, knights used body armor and helmets for protection. But with their faces covered, they couldn't tell who was who. You could battle an enemy only to find out that you were fighting your friend.

**1.** With a rolling pin, flatten a handful of clay to make a base about 15 cm x 15 cm (6 in. x 6 in.) and 1 cm (1/2 in.) thick.

**2.** Place the base on a cookie sheet. Carefully trim the edges with your knife so the base outline is the shape you want. Remove the cuttings.

**3.** Mold leftover clay pieces into the 3-D forms of your main design. Score the underside of each piece with a fork.

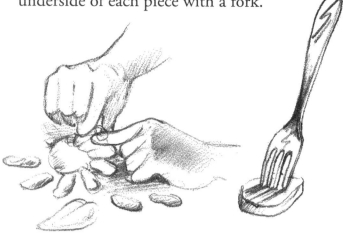

**4.** Press the forms firmly onto the base and smooth all edges to be sure the forms stick on well.

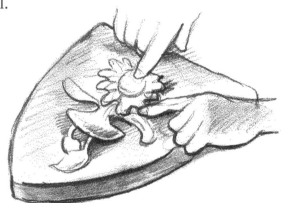

**5.** If your crest is made of baking clay, follow the directions on page 156 for drying.

**6.** When the crest has hardened, paint it and add decorations.

Knights started to decorate their shields with personal symbols so their friends could recognize them.

Because the symbols had to be clear from a distance, they were simple designs drawn in strong colors.

Crests were repeated on their clothes, flags, saddle skirts and helmets.

# MEMORY LANE

**W**here did your grandparents grow up? What school did they go to? Who were their friends? If you have a grandparent who grew up near where you live, bring his childhood stories to life by taking a trip together to his old town or neighborhood.

## PLANNING AHEAD

- Set a date for when you and your grandparent are free.

- Decide where you're going, how to get there and how long to stay.

- Write or phone the local tourist bureau about accommodation, if there are no old friends or family to stay with.

- Get a current map of the area and plan what you want to see.

## WHAT TO DO?

Tour the old neighborhood and find your grandparent's home. Draw or take a picture of what that home looks like now. Has it stayed the same or been torn down and replaced with a totally different building? When you're touring, look for a natural souvenir. Take home an acorn or maple key and plant a new tree from your ancestral roots.

Check out the school. Ask at the office if you can look through the halls. Can you find your grandparent's name on the wall plaques? There's Granddad pictured with the football team of 1948.

Where did your grandparent hang out? The candy store? The movie theater? The park? Together, you can buy some candy, see a movie or picnic in the same park.

## SPOT THE DIFFERENCES

Compare then and now with old photos. Look for changes in styles such as clothing, hairstyles and cars. The world will be different now too — keep an eye out for bigger trees, renovated or replaced buildings, satellite dishes and advertising signs.

# STONE RUBBING

Add to the tour of your grandparent's childhood with a trip to the local cemetery. Find the gravestones of your relatives and record the information on them for your family tree (see page 12). Get permission at the church to make a rubbing of an ancestor's stone, which you can then hang up at home.

**YOU'LL NEED**

a large piece or roll of white craft paper

scissors

masking tape

a gray, black, gold or silver crayon

a pen

an elastic band

**1.** Find a relative's gravestone that has an interesting design. Cut a piece of paper that will cover the face of the stone. Tape it in place.

**2.** Carefully rub the crayon over the paper, stroking in one direction with even pressure. If you rub back and forth, you may tear the paper.

**3.** When you are finished, remove the paper from the stone. Write the date on a piece of tape and stick it to the back of the rubbing. Roll it up and hold in place with an elastic band. Remove all tape from the tombstone.

# TOMBSTONE TALES

While you're in the graveyard, check out other tombstones. The dates and names may remind your grandparent of interesting childhood stories. They tell of tragedies, epidemics, war and infant deaths in the times before modern medicine. These events may help you understand what life was like when your grandparents were kids.

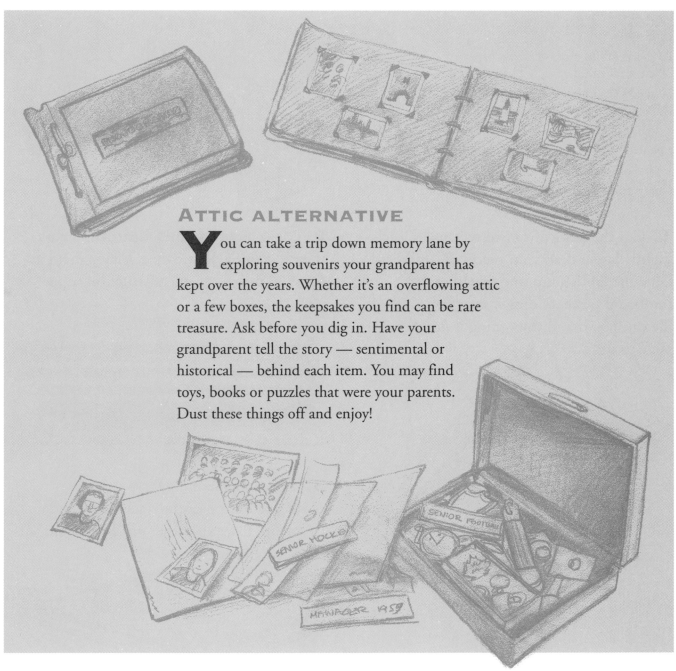

## ATTIC ALTERNATIVE

Y ou can take a trip down memory lane by exploring souvenirs your grandparent has kept over the years. Whether it's an overflowing attic or a few boxes, the keepsakes you find can be rare treasure. Ask before you dig in. Have your grandparent tell the story — sentimental or historical — behind each item. You may find toys, books or puzzles that were your parents. Dust these things off and enjoy!

# PHOTO ALBUM

**Y**our grandparents probably have family pictures collected in photo albums. They also may have drawers or boxes filled with pictures. Here is a way to make an album to show off and protect those loose photos. Make this with your grandparents, or give it to them as a gift.

| YOU'LL NEED |
| --- |
| scissors |
| 1 m (3 ft.) fabric, wallpaper or fancy wrapping paper |
| 2 sturdy sheets of cardboard, 22 cm x 28 cm (8½ in. x 11 in.) |
| white glue |
| 20 sheets of black construction paper 22 cm x 28 cm (8½ in. x 11 in.) |
| 20 sheets clear plastic, 22 cm x 28 cm (8½ in x 11 in.), to protect the photos (optional) |
| a ruler |
| a pencil |
| a one-hole punch |
| 1 m (3 ft.) ribbon or shoelace |

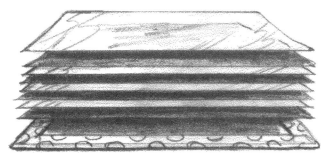

**1.** Cut the fabric into two rectangles, each slightly larger than your pieces of cardboard. Glue the fabric onto one side of each cardboard piece, folding it over the edges of the cardboard and smoothing it flat. Set them aside to dry.

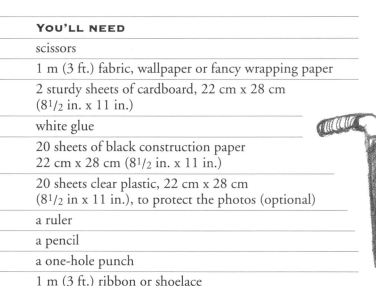

**2.** Make a stack of the construction paper sheets. If using plastic sheets, layer them in between the pieces of construction paper.

**3.** Place one piece of fabric-covered cardboard on top of the stack, fabric-side facing up. Place the other on the bottom, fabric-side facing down.

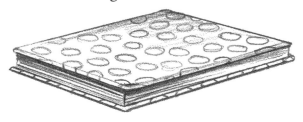

**4.** Straighten the stack and lay it horizontally in front of you. Measure 2.5 cm (1 in.) from the left edge of the card and make a vertical fold down the cardboard.

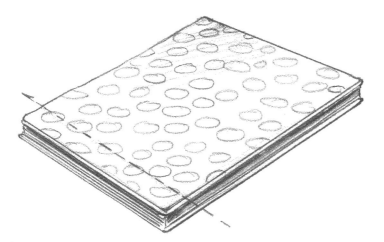

**5.** Make the same clean fold down every sheet of construction paper. Run the ruler along the folds to make them sharp. Open the folds and straighten the stack.

**6.** Mark two points down the left-hand edge of the cover. Center the points between the edge and fold line. Punch holes at those points through the covers and each sheet in the stack.

**7.** Thread your ribbon or shoelace through these holes and tie the ends in a bow.

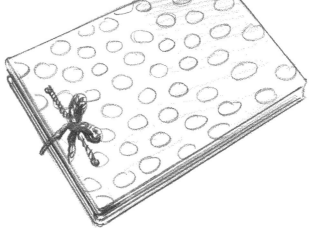

**8.** Turn the page for ideas about how to select and display the pictures in your album.

## OLD ALBUMS

Although old photo albums may be faded, they tell stories. Your forebears selected, ordered and labeled the photographs according to their own tastes and family history. Don't be tempted to spoil these family treasures by removing pictures.

# FAMILY PHOTOS

O nce you have an album to display family photographs (see pages 24–25), ask your grandparents to help you select pictures to put in it.

**YOU'LL NEED**

old photos

a fine-tipped marker

a glue stick

photo corners

a gold or silver marker

**1.** When you see a picture that interests you, ask who the people in it are, when it was taken and what the occasion was. Use a fine-tipped marker to print this information on the back.

**2.** With your grandparents' permission, choose photos to display in the album.

**3.** Arrange the photos in the album and paste them in using a glue stick and photo corners. Run glue around the edges and the center of the back of each photo. The photo corners will give the older photos extra protection. Leave space around each photo so it is framed by the construction paper.

**4.** With a gold or silver marker, write a caption below each picture using the information you collected in step 1.

**5.** Make a page that shows you, your parents and your grandparents all as babies. Think of other across-the-generations pages you can create — you could use photos taken at the beach, grade school classroom pictures or ones that show you and your relatives posing with pets.

## PHOTO FASHIONS

**W**hen you don't know the date of some photos, look for clues in the pictures:

- How are people posing? One hundred years ago, people posed with serious expressions. Nobody thought it proper to "say cheese."

- What are people wearing? Your grandparents will know when certain fashions were popular.

- How old are the people in the picture? If your great-grandmother was a toddler in the photo and she's 92 now, then the picture is about 90 years old.

- Where was the picture taken? Ask when the family lived in or visited that place.

- Is the photo in color? Color processing was invented in 1907, but not widely available for many years.

# FAMILY CALENDAR

**E**ach family has a calendar year of its own. Your birthdays, anniversaries and special days are unique to your family. Make a calendar for your grandparents that records these dates. This family calendar is for every year. So, unlike an ordinary calendar, there are no days of the week.

**YOU'LL NEED:**

13 sheets of construction paper, about 23 cm x 30 cm (9 in. x 12 in.)

a ruler

a pencil

a one-hole punch

paper-hole reinforcements

a sheet of clear plastic, 23 cm x 30 cm (9 in. x 12 in.)

scissors

a black fine-tipped marker

family photos

2 "O" rings

ribbon

**1.** At the top of each sheet of construction paper, make a mark 8 cm (3 in.) from each side and 2 cm (3/4 in.) from the top. Use a one-hole punch to make holes at the marks. Stick paper-hole reinforcements on both sides of each hole. Repeat this process with the sheet of plastic. Set one piece of construction paper and the plastic aside for a cover.

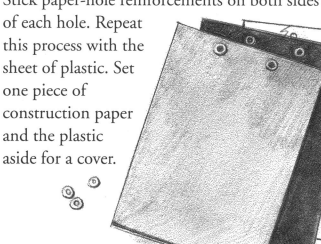

**2.** Starting at the bottom of each page, draw 15 lines, about 1 cm (1/2 in.) apart. Draw a line down the middle, creating 30 spaces.

**3.** Label each page with the name of a month, starting with January.

**4.** Fill in the days for each month, with 1 to 15 down the left-hand side and 16 to 30 on the right. When a month has 31 days, write 30 and 31 on the same line.

**5.** Record special family days throughout the year. Include such days for parents, siblings, grandparents, aunts, uncles, cousins and yourself.

**6.** Decorate the top half of each sheet with a picture of a "relative of the month." You might want to feature someone celebrating a birthday or if you have a great photo of your grandfather sailing, paste it on the July sheet.

**7.** Make a cover for the calendar and protect it with a plastic sheet. Hold it all together with two "O" rings. Tie a ribbon between the two rings to hang it up. Remove the rings to change the month.

# FAMILY PATCHWORK QUILT

**A**sk your grandparents, parents and siblings to contribute articles of clothing: Granddad's business shirt, Mom's sundress, baby's crib sheet, your faded jeans and flannel shirt. Pieced together into a quilt, they will create both warmth and memories. The instructions are for a twin-size quilt. You may decide to make a crib quilt or a king-size quilt. In any case, it's a long-term family project.

### YOU'LL NEED

a piece of cardboard, 11 cm x 11 cm (4$\frac{1}{2}$ in. x 4$\frac{1}{2}$ in.)

a pencil

a ruler

scissors

patterned and plain fabric pieces

an iron

a fine-tipped marker

masking tape

straight pins

a needle and thread

thin quilt batting or flannel material

a single-bed sheet

a darning needle

colorful wool or yarn

**1.** With the help of an adult, iron each piece of fabric.

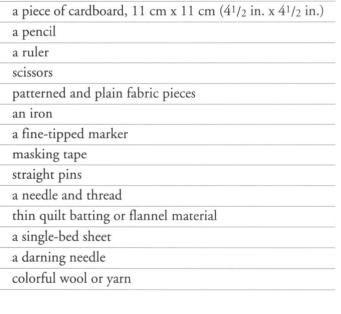

**2.** Place the cardboard square on the wrong side (inside) of the fabric and trace around it using a marker. Cut out each square. You'll need 324 squares: 162 cut from patterned fabric and 162 from plain fabric.

**3.** Lay the squares on the floor and arrange them in 18 rows of 18 squares so that they make a pleasing pattern. Place plain squares between patterned ones.

**4.** Collect each row in order and hold them together with straight pins. Using tape, number the fabric piles 1 through 18.

**5.** To sew the first row, place the second square on top of the first, with right sides (the outside) of the fabric together. Pin along the side of the square. Sew a 0.5 cm (1/4 in.) seam down the pinned side, using a running stitch or sewing machine. Remove the pins.

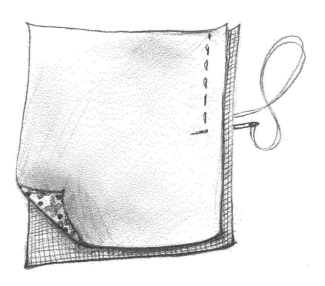

**6.** In the same manner, pin and sew the third square to the second. Continue until all 18 are sewn together. Set this row of squares aside and sew together the other 17 rows the same way.

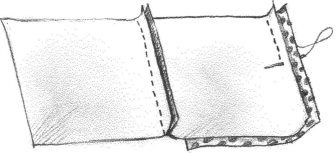

**7.** With right sides together, pin and sew the first and second rows together. Repeat until all 18 rows are sewn. Remove the tape.

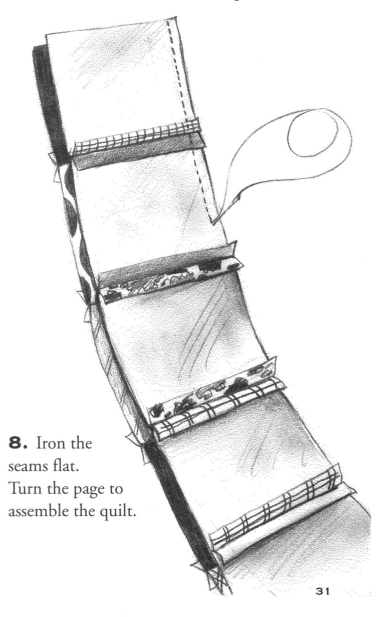

**8.** Iron the seams flat. Turn the page to assemble the quilt.

# QUILT ASSEMBLY

When the quilt top is sewn, you still need the batting and the backing to complete the project.

**1.** Baste together pieces of batting, making a piece the same size as the quilt top. Basting is done with brightly colored thread, in large, loose stitches. It is removed, if it shows, when the project is finished.

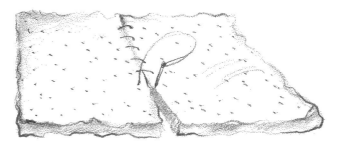

**2.** Place the batting on the wrong side of the quilt top and baste in place.

**3.** Lay the bed sheet on the floor and smooth it out. Place the basted quilt and batting on top of the sheet, right sides together. Trim away any excess sheet material.

**4.** Pin around the outside edges. Sew a 0.5 cm (1/4 in.) seam in running stitch, leaving a small opening of 15 cm (6 in.) in the middle of one end.

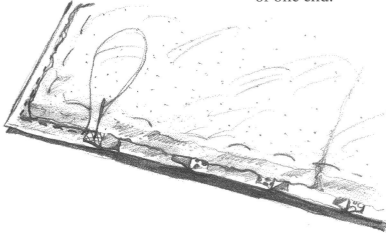

**5.** Turn the quilt right side out through the opening. Iron it flat. Tuck the edges of the opening inside and stitch shut with small stitches.

**6.** Lay the quilt on the floor and smooth it flat. Hold in place with 12 pins spaced around the quilt. Baste through all thicknesses around the pins. Remove the pins.

**7.** To finish the quilt, sew, then tie a piece of wool in the middle of each square as follows:

- Thread the darning needle with wool.

- Push the needle through the middle of the square from the right side of the quilt to the back, leaving 10 cm (4 in.) of wool on the right side.

- Make a new hole beside the first stitch and push the needle from the back to the front. Cut the second piece of wool to measure 10 cm (4 in.)

- Tie the two pieces of wool together in a double knot. Trim.

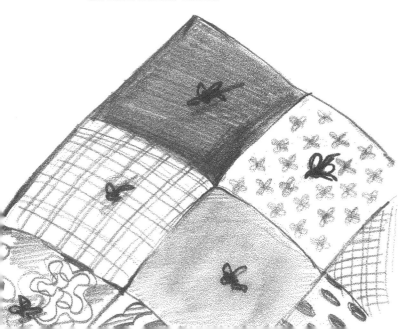

## TRADITIONAL QUILTING

Wool ties will hold the quilt together, but real quilting has more detailed sewing. If you want to complete your quilt the old-fashioned way, you'll need chalk, a thimble, a large embroidery hoop, thread and a sharp needle.

- Using a needle and thread, outline all the squares with small running stitches.

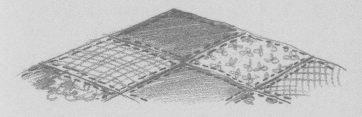

- With chalk, draw a simple pattern, such as a star, in the middle of each square.

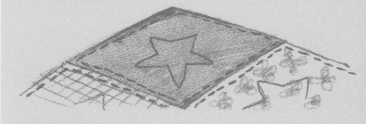

- Center and attach an embroidery hoop over the pattern.

- Make small, loose stitches through all layers along the chalk lines. The fabric should lie flat and not be pinched in or puckered.

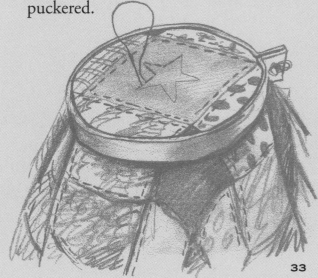

# FAMILY CROSSWORD

**Y**ou are connected to your relatives by stories, recipes, celebrations, mementos, secrets, holidays and other fun things. Here's a simple crossword puzzle that uses your family connections.

**1.** Write a list of family names. Include surnames and given names of your parents, grandparents, brothers, sisters, aunts, uncles, cousins and you.

**2.** Beside each name write a clue or definition. Include some tricky puns or riddles in the clues.

**3.** Draw a square crossword grid at least 10 spaces across and 10 spaces down — more if you have a big family or a family with long names.

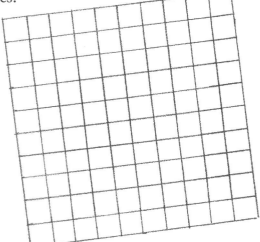

**4.** Write your own surname down or across the center of the grid. Then, position the other names so that each one intersects with at least one other. This may take some time and arranging.

**5.** After placing all your names, look at the grid to see if you can fill in other squares with family words — significant place names, recipes or names of pets. Write in these words and clues for them on your list from step 1.

**6.** Color in the empty spaces with pencil. Then, starting at the top left-hand square, number the used squares row by row, left to right. Only number the squares that start a word. This is your solutions page.

**7.** Make a clean copy of the puzzle. Draw an identical grid on the top of a second sheet of paper. Color and number the same squares as on the first grid. Do not write any letters in the squares.

Across
2. Likes to garden
5. Lives in Nelson, B.C.
8. Loves to swim
9. An uncle
10. A flower

Down
1.

**8.** Below the grid, on the left-hand side, write "Across" and on the right-hand side, "Down." Write your clues in the Across and Down lists, depending on whether the word runs across or down the grid. Before each clue, write the number of the square that contains the first letter of the word the clue refers to.

**9.** Try out your crossword puzzle on your grandparents. See if they make the same connections you do.

## NEWSPAPER CROSSWORD PUZZLES

If your grandparents love crosswords, here are some facts you can share:

- Crossword puzzles became popular in 1910 and newspapers started to print them — without solutions.

- In 1914, the *New York World* printed the first list of solutions and soon other newspapers did too.

# CROSS-STITCH EMBROIDERY SAMPLER

**O**ne hundred and fifty years ago children practiced needlework skills and learned their letters and numbers all in one activity. Today this is a craft activity you can share with a grandparent. Before you go to the craft store, see if your grandparent has any of the supplies.

**YOU'LL NEED**

graph paper

colored pencils

an iron

a piece of loosely woven cloth, such as aida cloth, 50 cm x 40 cm (20 in. x 16 in.)

a dress-marking pencil

a ruler

cotton embroidery thread

a sewing needle

scissors

**1.** Design your sampler on graph paper. Each square on the paper represents one cross-stitch. Letters should be seven squares high and three to four squares wide. Leave spaces between letters and symbols. Center your design in the middle of the paper. A border of your family crest or a fun pattern will complete the design. Use colored pencils to show the color of embroidery thread you wish to use for each letter or symbol.

**2.** With an adult's help, iron the cloth. Copy your graph paper design onto the center of the cloth, using a ruler to guide the dress-marking pencil.

**3.** Embroidery thread has six strands. Cut an arm's length piece of thread. Divide it into three pieces of two strands each. Set two aside and thread one piece through the needle. Double the thread and tie a knot at the end.

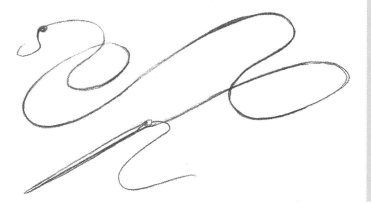

**4.** Make cross-stitches by pulling the needle from the back of the fabric to the front, beginning at the top left of the X. Poke the needle from front to back at the lower right corner. Pull through from behind. Complete the stitch by pulling the needle from the back top right corner and poke down through at the lower left corner.

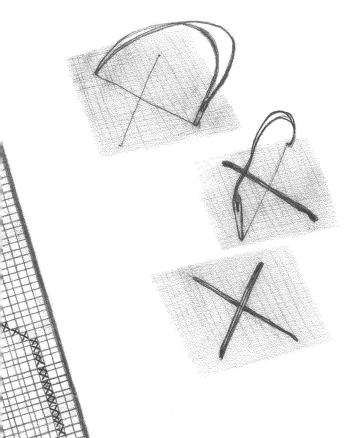

## FAMILY SAMPLER

Make a permanent record of your personal crossword (see page 34), with a cross-stitch sampler.

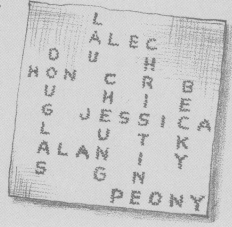

**5.** Make all the stitches this way. Always change the color or start a new strand of thread from the back of the fabric.

**6.** As a final touch, cross-stitch your name and the date on the lower right-hand corner. This will help future family historians.

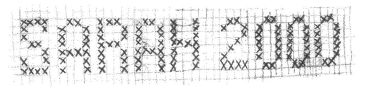

**7.** Frame your sampler, or hang it from a dowel.

# COLLECTIONS

**S**tarting a collection is a great hobby to share with a grandparent. There are lots of things you can collect and trade: bird feathers, stamps, maps, shells and rocks. Why not start with postcards? You can exchange them, get the thrill of receiving mail and display them on this neat board. Make one for each of you and help each other fill it.

### YOU'LL NEED

| |
|---|
| 2 pieces of heavy corrugated cardboard, 40 cm x 60 cm (16 in. x 24 in.) |
| a piece of heavy fabric, 45 cm x 65 cm (18 in. x 26 in.) |
| craft glue |
| a paintbrush |
| a stapler |
| ribbon |
| pushpins |

**1.** Glue the two pieces of cardboard together. Then brush one side with a thin coating of glue.

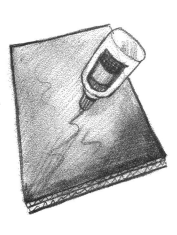

**2.** Smooth the fabric flat on a table. Place the glue side of the cardboard in the middle of the fabric. Press it down firmly.

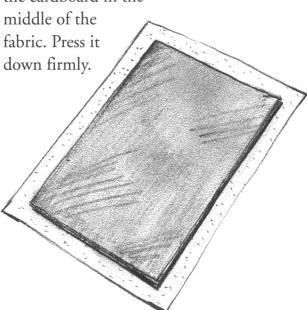

**3.** Fold the unglued edges of the fabric, like the corners of a parcel, onto the back of the cardboard. Staple the fabric in place.

# STAMP COLLECTING

In the past, stamp collections were not as exciting as they are now. Stamps were sorted by country and price and neatly pasted into books. Now stamps are colorful with amazing graphics and themes. You can collect all the celebrity stamps from countries around the world or choose another theme such as inventions, transportation, the Olympics or wildlife. When you are exchanging mail with your grandparents, look for interesting stamps.

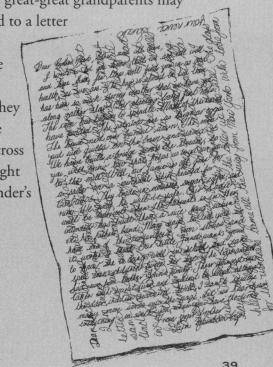

**4.** Tie ribbons together to form long lengths and criss-cross them over the fabric. Secure them in place with pushpins. Tuck postcards behind the ribbons.

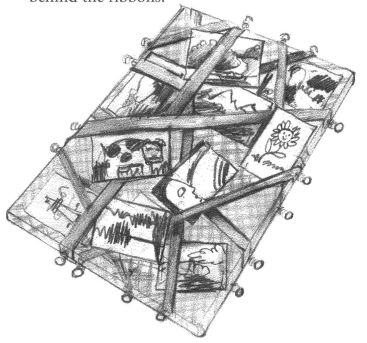

## COLLECTIVE MEMORIES

Have your grandparents saved any letters from your great-great relatives? If so, you can read your forebears' stories in their own words. You'll get a feeling for the times they lived in from their handwriting, the way they greeted people and the slang they used. To save money on paper, your great-great grandparents may have replied to a letter by writing back on the one they received. They often wrote sideways across the page, right over the sender's words.

# GROWING CONCERNS

**"L**ook how you've grown!" You've probably heard that hundreds of times, but your grandparents love to celebrate how much you have grown. Their home is the perfect place to hang a height chart and record how much taller each family member gets every year.

## YOU'LL NEED

a roll of paper about 2.2 m x 10 cm (7 ft. x 4 in.) (adding-machine paper or shelf paper work well)

a ruler

a pencil

colored markers

thumbtacks

a cardboard tube (optional)

masking tape (optional)

**1.** Unroll the paper. Draw a straight line the length of the paper, down the middle. Starting from the bottom use your ruler and markers to mark off inches and feet up one side of your midline and centimeters and meters up the other side. Put a title at the top such as "Height Chart" or "Our Growing Family."

**2.** With your grandparent's permission, tack the height chart inside a closet or utility room door. Be sure the bottom of the chart touches the floor. (If it is not possible to tack up your chart, store the roll in a labeled cardboard tube. Take it out and tape it lightly in a doorframe for a day at a time.)

**3.** At a family gathering, stand all your relatives, one at a time, with their backs to the chart. Draw a pencil line to indicate each person's height. Beside each line, write the date and the person's name and age. Don't forget to ask someone to mark your height too.

**4.** Every following year, update your height chart.

## FAMILY SIZE

You will likely grow taller than your grandparents or great-grandparents. That is because when you were a baby your parents knew more about good nutrition for children than was known when your grandparents were young. However, you will probably be the same general size as your grandparents. If they are tall people, you will be tall too. Ask your grandparents if height or size has had any effect on their lives. Did your forebears do certain work or play specific sports because of their height?

# PROFILE PORTRAITS

**S**ilhouettes made attractive family portraits before cameras were common. Lined up in a row, they showed off interesting similarities and differences between family members. Make profile portraits of your family and compare everyone's features.

**YOU'LL NEED**

a lamp or flashlight

masking tape

paper

a pencil

scissors

glue

black construction paper

**1.** Have your grandparent sit on a chair between the lamp or flashlight and a wall. The chair should be angled so that a profile of the face appears as a shadow on the wall. You may have to draw the curtains to darken the room.

**2.** Tape the paper on the wall where the shadow falls and draw the outline of the profile on the paper.

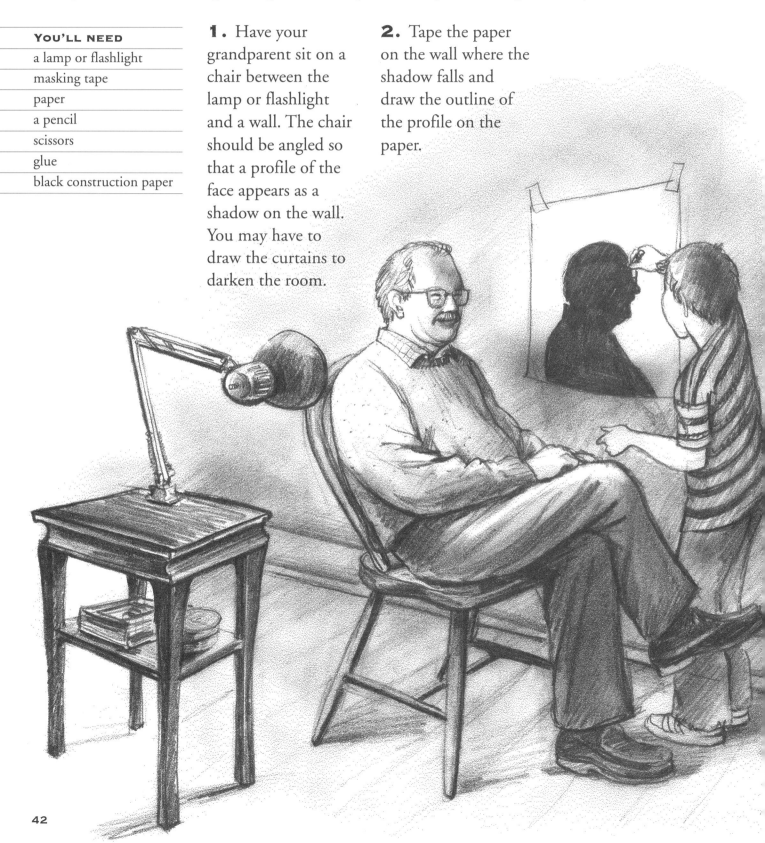

**3.** Turn off the lamp and remove the paper. Cut out the profile and glue it onto the black construction paper.

**4.** Now have a grandparent trace your profile.

**5.** Display the profiles side by side for easy comparison.

## FAMILY GENES

**B**ig noses, long middle toes, blue eyes and even allergies are characteristics that are passed on from grandparents and parents to biological kids. So is the ability to cross your eyes, wiggle your ears or roll your tongue. Sometimes these traits skip a generation and show up later. Ask your grandparents what traits run in your family that you may pass on to your children.

# KEEPING IN TOUCH

**W**hen you and your grandparents are apart, you can send greetings and share news by phone or by sending each other cards, letters, faxes and e-mails. Another fun way to keep in touch is by mailing messages back and forth on audiotape.

## STORY-TAPING TIPS

**1.** Jot down on paper what you want to tape. Consider making a tape that includes a variety of items such as:

- a new song
- an interview with your parents
- a story from your day
- a good joke
- a movie or book review
- a poem you learned in school
- the play-by-play of your sister's soccer goal.

**2.** Think up ways to dramatize your message and practice. Can you add feeling by raising your voice, whispering or leaving meaningful pauses? Can you add sound effects? When you come up with an especially good word or phrase, jot it down so you won't forget it.

**3.** Make the tape. Use the pause button when you take breaks, lose your place or want to add special effects.

**4.** At the end of the message, suggest what your grandparents might tape for you. Ask about their childhood and you could get back a family story to treasure for years.

**5.** Place the tape in its case and wrap paper around it so the edges will not poke through. Send the tape by regular mail in a standard-sized envelope.

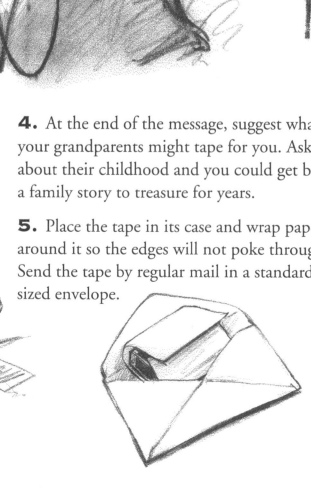

# THANK-YOU'S

Here's a great way to keep in touch and say thank-you for a great visit at the same time. Before your stay is over, hide notes on small slips of paper around your grandparents' house, in their suitcase or car. Think up one-liners and smart places to tuck them.

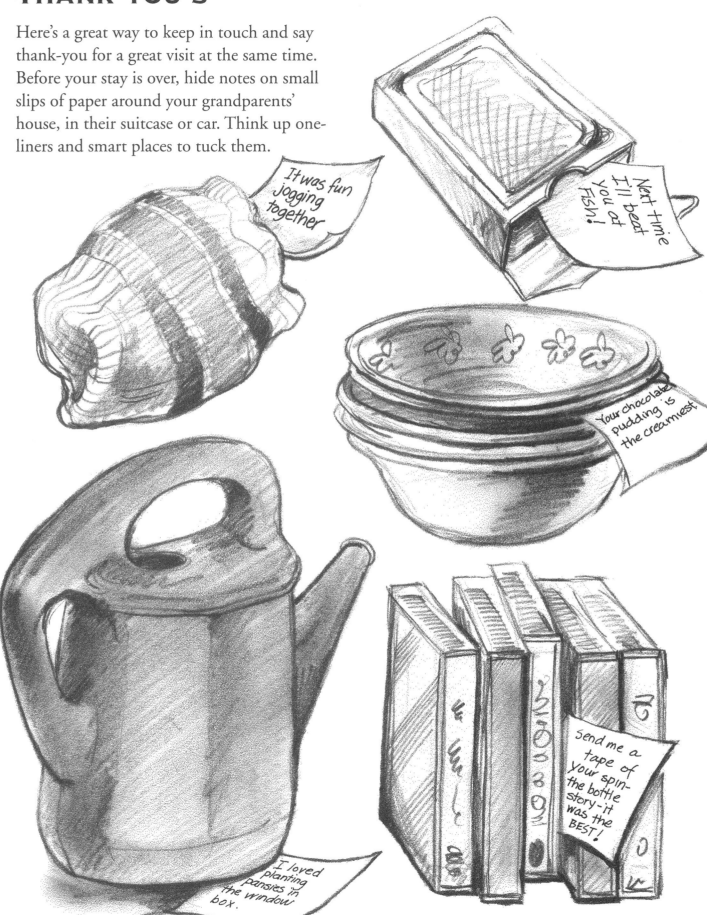

It was fun jogging together

Next time I'll beat you at fish!

Your chocolate pudding is the creamiest

I loved planting pansies in the window box.

Send me a tape of your spin-the-bottle story—it was the BEST!

# FUN AND GAMES

**P**lay the traditional games described in this section with your grandparents and they may remember variations or totally different games they can teach you.

You may recognize an

older game and be able

 to show your grandparents

the modern way to play it.

 Soon you'll

have a big

   selection of games you can share

with family

and friends.

# PARLOR GAMES

**W**hen your grandparents were kids, their grandparents may have displayed the best furniture and ornaments in a room called the parlor. Children were allowed to enter only on special occasions and had to be on their best behavior. Any family games that were played in the parlor had to be quiet so none of the treasures were broken. See if your grandparents remember some parlor games. Together, you can try to think of the modern versions.

## CATEGORIES

This game is for two or more players, each supplied with a pencil and paper.

**1.** Players draw square charts on their own papers. Each chart has four boxes across and down.

**2.** Players agree on four categories such as names, snacks, pets and games. Players print one category above each column on their charts in the order decided by the group.

**3.** Everyone agrees on a four-letter word, such as "home," and writes it down the side of the chart, with one letter of the word starting each row.

**4.** Players then work alone and try to print a word in each box that starts with the letter at the beginning of the row, but in the category at the top of the column.

**5.** After five minutes, everyone stops to score. Players call out their words and get two points for a correct word that no one else used, and one point for a word others used. The player with the highest score wins.

**6.** For a more advanced game, everyone increases the number of categories (across the chart) and the length of the word (down).

## 20 QUESTIONS

The first player thinks of a person or a thing that is familiar to the other player or players. The others are allowed to ask up to 20 questions to find out what the first player is thinking. The first player can only answer "yes," "no" or "sometimes."

It is a good idea to ask broad questions first and then narrow them down — "Is this a person?" "Is this person alive?" "Is this person a woman?" If the person or thing is guessed before the 20 questions are asked, the player who guesses correctly begins the next round.

A variation of this game is animal, vegetable and mineral. The first player thinks of a subject and describes it as animal, vegetable or mineral. The game then continues in the same way as 20 questions.

# CONCENTRATION

Two or more people can play this memory game. You need a set of tiles such as Scrabble pieces or dominoes, or playing cards.

**1.** Pair up as many tiles or cards as you can. If you use Scrabble pieces, choose at least 8 letter-pairs — 2 a's, 2 b's, 2 c's and so on. If you use domino tiles, select at least 8 different combinations and then find 8 identical tiles so each of the 16 tiles has a twin.

**2.** Turn the tiles or cards facedown on a table and mix them around.

**3.** Each player, in turn, overturns 2 tiles. When a player finds a pair, the player gets to keep it and try again. If the 2 tiles do not match, the player turns them facedown again, exactly where they were, and the next player takes a turn.

**4.** Players take turns until all tiles have been paired and collected. The winner is the one with the most tiles at the end.

# SPIN THE BOTTLE

When your grandparents were young, the most embarrassing parlor game was spin the bottle. Players sat in a circle with a bottle in front of them. Each player took a turn spinning the bottle and whomever the narrow end of the bottle pointed to when it came to rest was supposed to kiss the spinner. That person could tell a story or sing a song instead of kissing — if he or she wished. See if your grandparents have any memories of this game.

# TRAY GAME

Two or more players can play this game, each with a pencil and paper. You also need a tray and a number of small objects.

**1.** One player secretly chooses an assortment of small objects and places them on the tray.

**2.** The player shows the tray to the others for one minute and then hides or covers the tray.

**3.** The players write down on their pieces of paper what they remember seeing on the tray.

**4.** The person who remembers the most wins.

# SING-ALONG

End an evening of parlor games by singing old favorites. If you are celebrating your grandparents' anniversary or another big event, add a modern touch to the sing-along. Change the words of a well-known song and tell the story of their lives.

# PENCIL AND PAPER GAME

**M**any board games you buy today started out as pencil and paper games. Here's an old pencil and paper game for two players that is now sold as a fancy board game. In this game, you and your opponent hide drawings of objects from each other. Try to find your opponent's objects first.

**YOU'LL NEED**

2 sheets of graph paper

2 pencils

2 red pens or pencils

a ruler

**1.** On the top half of each sheet of graph paper draw a square 10 lines across and 10 lines down. Draw an identical square on the bottom half of each sheet. On each square, label spaces between the lines across the top 1 to 10 and the spaces down the side "a" to "j." Name the top square on each sheet "mine" and the bottom "yours."

**2.** Give one sheet to your opponent and keep one for yourself. You and your opponent now choose symbols to represent the objects you plan to hide. Record the symbols down one side of your graph paper. Traditionally, you hide ships from each other, and different sizes of ships are symbolized by filling in different numbers of squares in a row. But you can choose another category of objects such as airplanes or gems. If you are hiding airplanes, for instance, you may decide that each player can have two 747s four spaces long, two DC-10s three spaces long and three helicopters two spaces long.

**3.** Sit across from your opponent at a table and set up a book between you so you can't see each other's paper. In the top square of your sheet, draw the objects you are hiding.

**4.** Try to find your opponent's hidden objects. Take turns calling coordinates (for example, c-3 or a-7). Each time you call a coordinate, mark it in pencil on the bottom square on your sheet. When you "guess" part of a hidden object, your opponent calls "hit" and you circle that pencil mark in red. Then you call out another coordinate to find more of that hidden object. If you "hit" again, you get another turn, but as soon as you miss, your opponent calls "miss" and you lose the turn.

**5.** The first player to find all the other player's hidden objects wins.

## MORE GAMES TO PLAY

**W**hich modern board games did your grandparents know in simpler, pencil and paper versions?

53

# TOOTHPICK TEASERS

**H**ere are some challenges that use only toothpicks. Ask your grandparents if they know any other toothpick puzzles. See page 160 for the answers.

## Puzzle 1

Arrange 12 toothpicks in four squares as shown. Now move 3 toothpicks to make three squares, still using all 12 toothpicks.

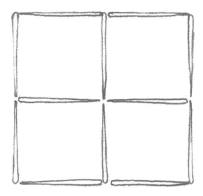

## Puzzle 2

Arrange 24 toothpicks to make nine squares as shown. Take away 8 toothpicks and leave only two squares.

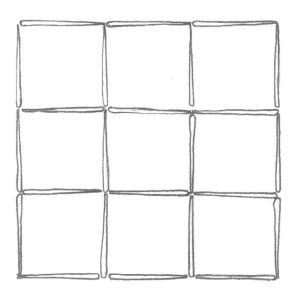

## Puzzle 3

Take 6 toothpicks of equal length and make four equilateral triangles.

## Puzzle 4

Place 6 toothpicks parallel to each other, with a space between each as shown. Without moving any, add 5 toothpicks to make 9.

# THE GAME OF NIM

This thousand-year-old Chinese game for two players uses only toothpicks. A parlor game in your grandparent's youth, now some people play NIM on the Internet. The idea behind NIM is to set up your opponent so he has to pick up the last toothpick.

To play the basic game, you'll need 16 toothpicks. Arrange the toothpicks in one row. Players take turns picking up 1, 2 or 3 toothpicks at a time. The player to pick up the last stick loses.

A modern variation uses 16 toothpicks arranged in four rows and columns as shown. Players take turns taking up to 4 toothpicks from the same row or column, as long as the toothpicks are next to one another. The player to pick up the last stick loses.

# TANGRAMS

Tangrams were invented in ancient China. Over the years they have been used in storytelling. The storyteller makes a tangram to show the main character in the story and then changes the pieces around to represent new characters or objects. You can invent and tell a tangram story yourself. If your grandparents do not have a ready-made tangram puzzle, you can make one.

**YOU NEED**

a pencil

paper

scissors

**1.** A tangram begins as a square that is cut into a pattern of seven pieces. Each piece is called a tan. Trace the tans on this page onto your paper and cut them out.

**2.** Mix them all around on a tabletop and then put them back together to make the square. If they do not fit, try flipping over the tan in the shape of a parallelogram.

**3.** Now you are ready to make a tangram picture. All seven tans must be used to make each tangram picture. The tans must touch each other, but may not overlap. Answers are on page 160.

**4.** Once you have gotten the hang of making tangram pictures, invent your own forms and take turns transforming someone else's pictures.

## TRANSFORMATIONS

**R**obots that transform, or "morph," are popular in cartoons today. Stories with animals that transform have been around since ancient times. One famous collection of these stories is *Metamorphoses* by a Roman named Ovid. Ask your grandparents if they can tell you an old transformation story that you can illustrate with tangrams.

# VANISHING ACTS

**D**o your grandparents have magic tricks up their sleeves? If they are true magicians, they will never share their secrets except with other magicians. Here are some tricks to practice for your grandparents.

## VANISHING SALTSHAKER

This is a trick to perform at the dinner table. You'll need a quarter, a saltshaker and a cloth napkin.

**1.** Place the quarter on the table and say, "I can make this coin disappear."

**2.** Cover it with the saltshaker, then cover both with the napkin.

**3.** Grasp the napkin with the saltshaker, lift them up and say, "Look, the coin has disappeared." Of course, the quarter is still there. Quietly pull the napkin and saltshaker over your lap and release your grip so the saltshaker falls into your lap. Keep hold of the napkin as if the shaker were still in it.

**4.** Say, "Wait. It's not the coin that disappears." Place the napkin over the coin and let go. Slap the napkin flat and say, "It's the saltshaker!"

# DISAPPEARING COIN

Hold a coin on the outstretched fingers of one hand. Sit down and rest your hand holding the coin on a table. Place your other hand on your chin and lean forward so that your elbow touches the table.

**1.** Say, "I will make this coin disappear." Rub the coin into your other arm above your elbow, holding the coin so your fingers completely cover it.

**2.** Pull your fingers away so the coin clatters to the table. Say, "Oh, it didn't work. I'll try again."

**3.** Drop both hands to pick up the coin. Pretend to pick the coin up with the same hand as before, but actually retrieve it with the other.

**4.** Quickly place your elbow back on the table and start rubbing your fingers into your arm, pretending you are rubbing in the coin. Meanwhile put the hand with the coin in it slightly over your shoulder. Place the coin on the back of your neck.

**5.** Stop rubbing your arm, pull away your hand and say, "See, it's disappeared." Show both empty hands.

**6.** Now, slowly stretch the arm that you supposedly pushed the coin into. Say, "Ooo, it's traveling up inside." Then, reach up and pull the coin off the back of your neck. Without smiling, say, "That feels better."

# CARD TRICKERY

H ere are some card tricks to dazzle a family audience.

## THE WHISPERING QUEEN

**1.** Pick up a deck of cards and say, "I need the queen of hearts for this trick." As you search for that queen, memorize the cards second and third from the bottom, in that order.

**2.** Place the queen faceup on a table and the rest of the deck facedown.

**3.** Ask one spectator to cut the deck in half and to place the top half, facedown, beside the queen. Then ask that person to count the number of cards in the bottom half, without looking at them. When people count cards, they usually reverse the order, so the cards you memorized should now be second and third from the top of the pile. If the person did not count that way, then re-count yourself to double-check the number, reversing the order of the cards as you count.

**4.** Ask a spectator to take the top card and then the bottom card and put them in the middle of the pile. Then ask someone to take the new top card (the first card you memorized) and put it in a pocket. Ask a second spectator to take the next card (the second card you memorized) and put it in another pocket.

**5.** Pick up the queen of hearts, touch the first pocket with the queen and place her near your ear. Ask her to whisper the name of the first card and then say it aloud. Repeat for the second card.

# SPELLING THE CARDS

**1.** Before performing, take 13 cards of one suit from a deck. Pile the cards facedown, in the following order starting with the bottom card: 5, 9, 10, king, jack, 2, 4, 6, queen, ace, 7, 8 and finally 3 on top.

**2.** Announce, "I will spell these cards."

**3.** Take the top card and pass it to the bottom of the pile and say, "o." Move the next card to the bottom saying "n" and the next saying "e." Turn up the fourth card, which will be the ace, place it in front of you and say "one."

**4.** Now spell "t-w-o," moving the top card to the bottom with each letter. Turn over the next card and lay it beside the ace and say, "two."

**5.** Continue spelling "t-h-r-e-e, three" and so on until you have one last card — the king.

# FAMILY TIE-UPS

Your grandparents may remember magic shows where magicians like Houdini attempted sensational disappearing stunts. But magic can be simple. Here are tricks that use nothing more than pieces of string or a scarf.

## STRINGS ATTACHED

For this trick, you'll need two volunteers and two pieces of ribbon or string, each about 1 m (3 ft.) long. The trick is easier if the strings are different colors.

**1.** Tie the ends of one string loosely around the wrists of one volunteer, so she can hold her hands comfortably apart.

**2.** Tie one end of the second string to one wrist of the second volunteer. Wind the free end of that string over and under the string tying the first volunteer's wrists together. Then tie the free end to the second volunteer's other wrist.

**3.** Challenge the two volunteers to separate themselves from each other without untying any knots, cutting the strings or slipping the strings off their wrists.

**4.** Show them the way to escape only when they give up. One volunteer takes the other's string and passes it through the loop around one of her own wrists, starting from her own body side. She must be careful not to tangle the strings. Then she keeps pulling the other volunteer's string through the loop until she can slip it over her own hand and pull free.

# CROSS KNOT

All you need for this trick is a scarf. Challenge anyone to tie a knot in the scarf so that one hand holds one corner, the other hand holds the opposite corner and neither hand lets go of its corner during the knotting.

The secret is to lay the scarf on a flat surface. Then with your arms crossed over your chest, bend forward and grab the corners of the scarf. Stand up uncrossing your arms. You will tie a knot in the scarf without letting go!

# LOST LOOPS

All you need for this trick is a piece of string about 1 m (3 ft.) long.

**1.** Make a loop in the middle of the string by crossing one end over the other. Tie the loop loosely with a half-knot. Let the loop dangle down, held by your half-knot, and hold up the ends of the string in your two hands.

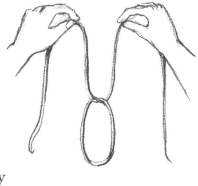

**2.** Make a second loop above the first loop and then tie the ends of the string into several full knots.

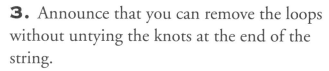

**3.** Announce that you can remove the loops without untying the knots at the end of the string.

**4.** Place the string behind your back, put your thumbs inside the bottom loop and pull them apart. The half-knot you made will slide up and join the other knots at the top and will seem to disappear.

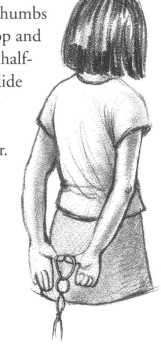

# WORD MAGIC

**B**ecome a word magician and try these twisters and teasers on your grandparents. They may know some to share with you too.

## TONGUE TWISTERS

Say these tongue twisters slowly and clearly. Repeat them several times, picking up the pace. Did they slur beyond recognition or did you dissolve into giggles?

- How much wood would a woodchuck chuck if a woodchuck could chuck wood?

- The skunk said the stump stunk. The stump said the skunk stunk. The skunk stunk. The stump stunk. The skunk and the stump stunk.

## RELATIVE RIDDLES

Can you piece together the family relationships in these riddles? Check page 160 for the answers.

**1.** Two fathers and two sons went fishing and they each caught a fish. They brought home three fish. How can this be true?

**2.** Two women are walking through the mall and a boy passes them. One of the women speaks to the boy. The other woman asks, "Do you know that boy?" "Yes," she says, "That boy's mother was my mother's only daughter." How are the two related?

**3.** If your aunt's brother is not your uncle, what relation is he to you?

# PIG LATIN

It's fun to share secret plans with a grandparent and no one else. If you both know a secret code, you can speak or write to each other in private. Then you can plan events or visits and surprise the rest of the family. Create a code of your own, or use pig latin.

- Move the first letter of a word to the end and add "ay." "Family" becomes "amily-fay."

- When a word begins with two or more consonants, these letters are moved to the end, followed by "ay." "Granny" becomes "anny-gray" (no comment on her hair color!).

- When a word begins with a vowel, the first letter doesn't move but "way" is added to the end. "Adult" becomes "adult-way."

# CARD GAMES

**H**ave fun with these card games — when it's just the two of you or with other family members as well.

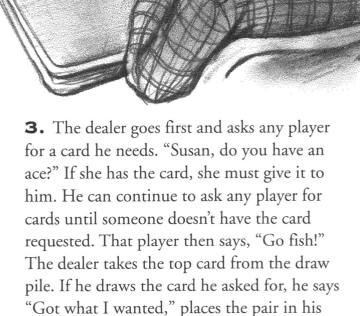

## FISH

Teach your grandparents how to play this simple game for two or more players. It won't take them long to catch on, but if they flounder, you'll net the most fish. The object of the game is to have the most pairs when all the cards have been paired.

**Playing the game**

**1.** Deal out seven cards for each player. Place the remaining cards, the draw pile, facedown on the table.

**2.** Match up any pairs in your hand and put them aside on the table in a pair pile, facedown.

**3.** The dealer goes first and asks any player for a card he needs. "Susan, do you have an ace?" If she has the card, she must give it to him. He can continue to ask any player for cards until someone doesn't have the card requested. That player then says, "Go fish!" The dealer takes the top card from the draw pile. If he draws the card he asked for, he says "Got what I wanted," places the pair in his pair pile and draws again.

**4.** The person to his left goes next.

## FISH II

Make the game more complicated by collecting four of a kind instead of pairs. This takes longer and there'll be more squawks and yells as players are asked to part with their cards.

# SNAP!

Has your grandparent got a drawer full of old cards — two or more decks with a few cards missing from each? Mix them together to make the perfect snap deck for two or more players.

**Playing the game**

**1.** Deal out all the cards. Leave the cards facedown as draw piles, one in front of each player.

**2.** Ready, set, go. Players turn over one card each, at the same time and place the card faceup in a pile next to their draw pile.

**3.** This is repeated until two cards of the same value are turned up. The first person who says "snap" wins all the faceup cards. These are placed facedown at the bottom of his draw pile.

**4.** Play continues as before. When all the cards in a player's draw pile have been turned faceup, the player leaves the top card faceup on the table and turns the rest of the cards over, making a new draw pile. The game continues until one person has all the cards.

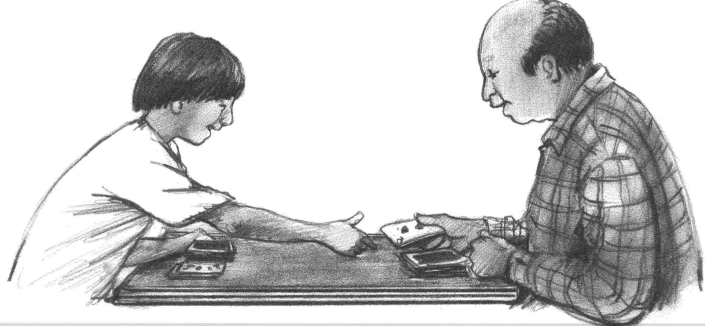

# ANIMAL SNAP

Crank up the fun and noise level by assigning each player an animal such as a pig, dog or cow. Instead of saying "snap," players must make their noise — oink, bark or moo. The first player to make his noise gets all the faceup cards. If a player gets mixed up and makes the wrong animal noise or says "snap," he loses all the cards in his faceup pile to the player who made the first correct noise.

# CRIBBAGE FOR TWO

C ribbage is a game your grandparents may have learned when they were young. Refresh their memories if they've forgotten or learn to play together.

## THE BOARD AND PEGS

The cribbage board records the score. There are usually two rows (one for each player) of 120 holes, plus start and finish holes. One player has two pegs of one color, the other player has two pegs of the other color for scoring.

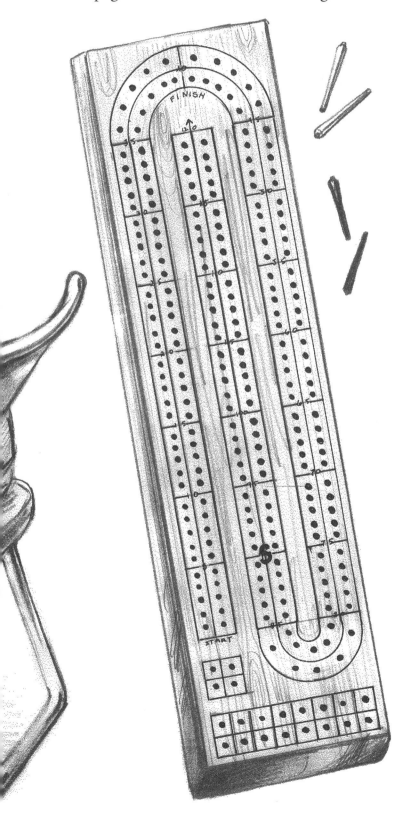

## DEALING

The dealer shuffles and deals six cards to both players. The rest of the deck is placed facedown in a pile.

## SCORING

The object of the game is to be the first player to complete the circuit of the board by scoring 120 points. In each hand, cards can be part of several different scoring groups. Think of all the possible combinations. The points are scored as follows:

- Two or more cards of any suit that add up to 15 = 2 points

- Two cards of the same number value = 2 points

- A jack turned up as a starter card = 2 points for the dealer

- A run of four cards of any suits = 4 points

- Four cards of the same suit, called a "flush" = 4 points

- Four cards of the same suit as the starter card = 5 points

- Three of a kind = 6 points

- Four of a kind = 12 points

## THE CRIB

Sort your cards, keeping in mind how to score points. Four cards become your hand and two are discarded in a pile called the crib. The dealer gets the crib. If you are the dealer, it's okay to give yourself good crib cards. If you're the opponent, try not to give away points (e.g., two 3s). The four cards in the crib are placed facedown on the table.

## CUTTING

The opponent cuts the cards by lifting up part of the deck. The dealer turns over the top card on the stack and places it faceup on the table. This is the starter card. The remaining deck is set aside for the next deal.

## PEGGING

Each player has two pegs on the board. One marks the start of a move, the other marks the points gained. To begin, leave one peg in the end hole and move the other peg the number of points won in the hand. On the second hand, the peg marking the first hand is left in place and the peg from the end hole is moved forward. Pegging continues in a leapfrog manner until one peg reaches the end.

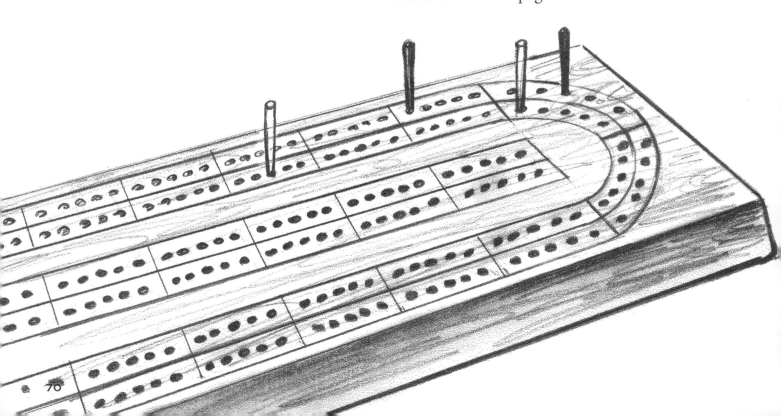

## PLAYING THE GAME

The opponent starts by laying down a card, faceup, while saying the value of the card. The dealer lays down a card, in a separate pile from his opponent, saying the total value of the opponent's card plus his own. If, for example, the two cards add up to 15 or make a pair, he says "for 2," meaning he gets 2 points. He then records his score with his first peg.

Players continue laying down in turns until the sum of the cards totals 31. If a player is unable to lay down (his cards will exceed the total of 31 or he has no cards left) he says "Go," giving his opponent the chance to score more points. When 31 is reached, or both players say "Go," the played cards are turned over and the process starts again from 0, until all eight cards have been played.

**Additional points:**

- The last playable card laid down totals exactly 31 = 2 points

- The last playable card laid down totals less than 31 = 1 point

- The last playable card laid down totals exactly 15 = 2 points for 15 and 1 point for last card

After the hands have been laid out together, each player picks up his hand. The opponent begins by counting as many combinations of points using her hand and the starter card. She records her points by pegging forward the correct number of spaces. The dealer does the same with his hand and with the crib. Then it's time to gather the cards, shuffle, deal, cut and continue playing.

# MARBLES

**P**ractice before you challenge your grandparents to a game of marbles. As kids, they may have played for hours to perfect their shots. Marbles are played for keeps. You win the game and you win the marbles. But, if you lose, you lose the marbles you played — until you can win them back.

## HOW TO SHOOT

**1.** Part of your hand must always touch the ground.

**2.** You can roll the marble or flick it with your thumb or finger, but with no forward movement of your hand.

**3.** You get better power if you "knuckle down":

- Put the knuckles of one hand on the ground with your palm facing your body.

- Curl your index finger to make a loose fist and place your thumb under the curl.

- Balance the marble on your thumbnail and then flick the thumb up to shoot the marble forward.

# SHOOT THE RING

On a patch of dirt, draw a circle about 1 m (3 ft.) across with a stick or the heel of your shoe. About 2 m (6 1/2 ft.) away, draw a shooting line.

**1.** Each player puts five or six marbles on the ring so the marbles are evenly spaced apart.

**2.** In turn, players shoot a different marble, called a shooter, from the line. The idea is to knock a marble off the ring.

**3.** If you successfully hit a marble off the ring, you win it.

**4.** If you do not knock a marble off the ring, you have to add your shooter to the ring

**5.** When all marbles are knocked off the ring, start over again.

## MARBLE COLLECTIONS

In your grandparents' time, marble collections included special and rare marbles. There were the beautiful ones such as cat's eyes, pure-ees (or peer-ees) and milk-ees. There were the powerful ones like steel-ees and boulders. Steel-ees were tiny, heavy and hard to shoot off the circle. Boulders were oversized and could take out lots of regular-sized marbles in one shot. With good shooting, players could win and add to their collections — and protect their favorite marbles at the same time.

# MORE MARBLE GAMES

## ALLEYWAYS

In this game, you prepare a series of targets and challenge players to shoot through them. Offer to give away marbles when players meet your challenge, and keep any marbles from missed shots.

**YOU'LL NEED**

a shoebox

scissors

a marker

**1.** Cut four arches out of the side of the box. One arch should be big enough for one marble to roll through when the box is turned upside down. The other three arches should be increasingly wider.

**2.** Write a number above each arch to show how many marbles you will give if a player can shoot through that arch.

**3.** Set the box upside down on a sidewalk or patch of bare ground. Draw a shooting line 2 m (6 1/2 ft.) from the box and invite all shooters to take up your challenge.

# JACKPOT

Dig a small hole, or "pot," in the ground with your heel. Then draw a shooting line about 2 m (6 1/2 ft.) from the hole.

**1.** Players take turns tossing a marble from the line toward the pot. The player whose marble lands closest gets to shoot first. If two or more marbles land in the pot, go to step 4.

**2.** Players take turns trying to get their marble to land in the pot.

**3.** When a marble lands in the pot, that player gets to take any marble that lands within a span of the pot. A span means the player can touch both the marble in the pot and the nearby marble by stretching the finger and thumb of one hand.

**4.** Should another marble land in the pot, the two players, starting with the first one in, get three turns to shoot each other out and win that marble and the place in the pot.

**5.** The game continues until all marbles are won and lost.

# BOMBS AWAY

Draw a circle in the dirt about 30 cm (1 ft.) across. Each player puts the same number of marbles inside the circle. Players take turns standing above the circle and dropping a "shooter" from eye level, trying to knock as many marbles as they can out of the circle. Players win any marbles they knock out and get their shooter back. If no marbles are knocked out, the shooter is added to the circle. The game continues until there are no marbles left in the circle.

# SHOOT SOME CARDS

Do you collect sports or movie cards? If they are kept looking as good as new, the cards can become more valuable. But when your grandparents were kids, it was more important to have a complete set of cards, dog-eared or not. Kids played with their duplicate cards, or "traders," to enlarge their collections. Use your traders to play these games with your grandparents.

## HOW TO SHOOT

- Grip one corner of a card between your pointer and middle finger. The length of the card runs parallel to your fingers and the card is held on the palm side of your hand.

- Practice an underhand flick, as that will give you more leaners (see lean-ees on the next page).

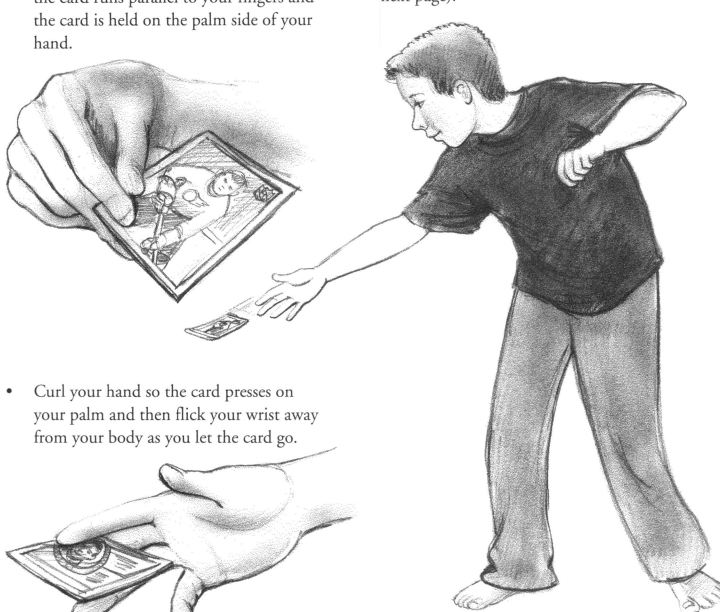

- Curl your hand so the card presses on your palm and then flick your wrist away from your body as you let the card go.

# HEADS OR STATS?

Players stand together, each holding one card at eye level. One player calls "heads" or "tails," and everyone drops his or her cards. Players check whose card lands heads (picture side) or tails (statistics side). If more than one player wins the call, they play a tiebreaker to find one winner. The winner gets all the cards dropped and also gets to start the game to follow, such as close-ees or lean-ees.

# CLOSE-EES

Players decide how many cards they will throw — maybe one, maybe five each. They stand at a shooting line about 3 m (10 ft.) from a wall. Players take turns throwing one card at a time, trying to place it with an edge touching or leaning on the wall.

The card closest to the wall wins when all cards have been played. Cards left leaning on the wall, called "leaners," win over cards lying flat and touching the wall. At the finish, if a leaner is leaning on another leaner, the outside "killer" leaner wins all.

# LEAN-EES

Lean several cards against a wall, side by side but not touching. Players stand 3 m (10 ft.) back and take turns shooting to make one fall. A successful player collects all the cards thrown so far as well as the fallen leaner. Then players start again and try to topple another leaner.

## NO BACKS-EES

When you shoot cards, you play for keeps. That means you can't change your mind and take back a card you played and lost.

# JACKS

J acks is a centuries old game, originally played with bones. All you need is a set of five jacks, a small bouncy ball and a flat, hard surface. Together with your grandparent learn each trick. Then challenge each other to a match.

## PLAYING THE GAME

Before playing, decide which tricks you will attempt and in what order. Decide who goes first by throwing all five jacks up in the air and catching as many as possible on the back of your hand. Then toss the caught jacks up again and try to catch them in the palm of your hand. Whoever ends up with the most jacks goes first. His turn is over if he fails to complete a trick properly. The first player to complete all the tricks is the winner.

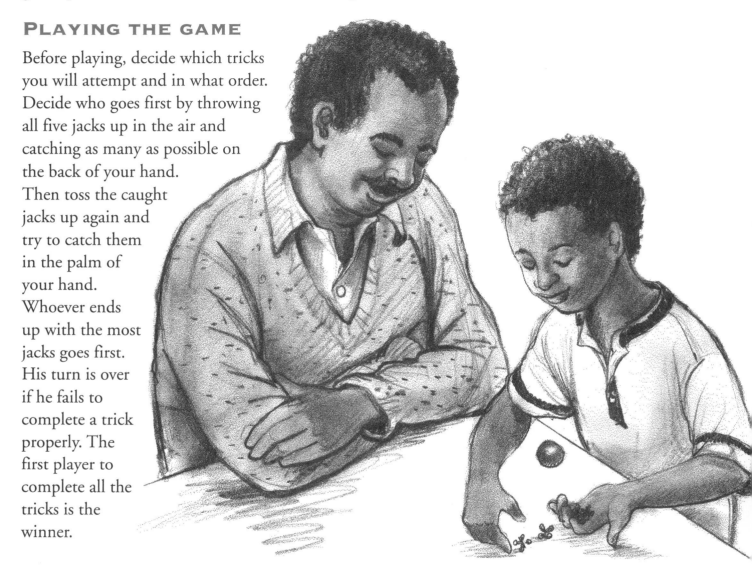

**You're out if:**

- you touch a jack you aren't trying to pick up
- you pick up too few, too many or drop any jacks
- you let the ball bounce more than once or drop it

**You're allowed to:**

- separate jacks that are stuck together if you are the first player to shout out "haystacks"
- throw the jacks again if you have a bad throw and you're first to shout "oversee"
- throw the ball again if it lands on a jack and you're first to shout "split jack"

## ONES

Throw the jacks on the ground. Using one hand, toss the ball into the air, pick up one jack and catch the ball after the first bounce. Transfer the jack to the other hand and repeat until all five jacks are picked up.

## TWOS, THREES, FOURS AND FIVES

Played as in Ones, jacks are picked up two, three, four and five at a time. In Twos, pick up two jacks twice, then one. In Threes, pick up three jacks, then two and so on. You can make the trick harder by starting with Fives and working backward to Ones.

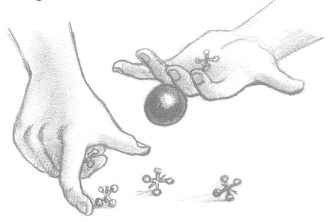

## JACKS IN A CAVE

Cup one hand and place it on the table, forming a cave. With the other hand, scatter the jacks. Play a game of Ones, but instead of picking up the jacks, flick or scoop them into the cave before the ball bounces twice. Try playing jacks in a cave with Twos, Threes, Fours and Fives too.

# SCHOOL-YARD GAMES

**W**hat game takes 15 minutes and uses equipment that fits in your pocket? A recess game! Show your grandparents what's hot in the school yard today. Then try these old-fashioned recess games they may have played. All you'll need is a yo-yo, a ball, sidewalk chalk and 2 m (6 1/2 ft.) of elastic.

## YO-YO

### BASIC YO-YO THROW

Learn the basic yo-yo throw and then try some tricks. Ask your grandparents if they know any others.

**1.** Slip the loop onto your middle finger and wind the string around the yo-yo. Hold the yo-yo with your thumb on one side, pointer finger in the middle and the remaining fingers on the other side.

**2.** Drop the yo-yo toward the ground. When it reaches the end of the string, give a little tug and lift up. The yo-yo will roll back up.

**3.** When it's almost back in your hand, lower your palm toward the ground. The yo-yo will go down again.

## YO-YO TIPS

- The tighter the thread is wound around the yo-yo, the faster it will go down and up.

- Yo-yo's don't work well if the string is twisted. Straighten the string by holding the loop with one hand and pulling down the length of the string with your thumb and first finger.

## FORWARD THROW

**1.** To throw the yo-yo straight out or up, tilt your wrist down, fingers up and swing up with your arm straight.

**2.** Make the yo-yo return by lowering your wrist and moving your arm back toward your body.

## SNOOZING YO-YO

**1.** Wind the string loosely around the yo-yo.

**2.** Do a basic yo-yo throw, but allow the yo-yo to spin with all the string played out — have a quick snooze.

**3.** Before the yo-yo stops spinning, lift your hand with a flick of the wrist and the yo-yo will return to your hand.

**4.** A forward throw followed by a snooze is another trick called a waterfall.

## WALKING THE DOG

**1.** To walk the dog, throw a snoozing yo-yo and lower your hand until the yo-yo touches the ground. Walk forward as the yo-yo rolls along the ground.

**2.** Before all the string is played out, lift the yo-yo off the ground and lift your wrist.

# YOKI

The object of the game is to complete a series of moves over a piece of elastic 2 m (6 1/2 ft.) long and 0.5 cm (1/4 in.) thick, while saying the yoki chant. Two people stretch the elastic between them at ankle level. The first player stands sideways to the elastic and says the yoki chant (see steps 1–5).

When the ankle level is completed, move the elastic to knee height, then to the heights of your waist, shoulder, head, and over the head. Each player's turn continues until she tangles her foot or cannot reach the elastic.

**1.** Yoki in the Kaiser (lift one foot over the elastic, touch the ground with your toe and return the foot to the starting position)

**2.** Yoki-I-dee-aay (repeat step 1)

**3.** Tank in da soda (repeat step 1)

**4.** Sadoo (jump over the elastic with both feet)

**5.** Sadday (jump back over the elastic to the starting position)

# BUTTON YO-YO

Don't have a yo-yo? Make a mini yo-yo and challenge your grandparent to see who can keep the yo-yo going the longest.

**YOU'LL NEED**

2 round 2.5-cm (1-in.) buttons with four holes

heavy-duty thread or strong, fine string

scissors

a needle

1 m (3 ft.) of polyester thread

**1.** Thread the needle with heavy-duty thread, double it and tie a knot at the end.

**2.** Hold the buttons, curved sides together. Sew back and forth across the buttons, forming an X in the middle, until the buttons are securely, but not too tightly, held together.

**3.** Secure the thread by inserting the needle under the X, pulling it all the way through and then pushing through the button several more times. Cut the thread.

**4.** Make a slip knot at one end of the polyester thread. Slide the knot between the two buttons and pull tight. Tie several plain knots to hold it in place. Trim off the short piece of thread.

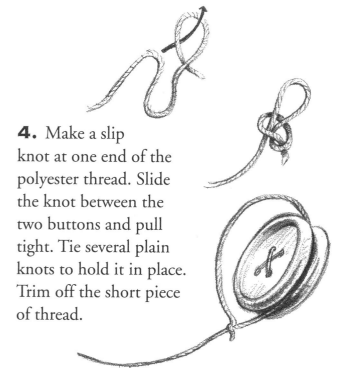

**5.** Wind the remaining thread between the two buttons. The thread should be snug but not too tight.

**6.** Hold the thread between your thumb and index finger and play as with a regular-sized yo-yo.

# HOPSCOTCH

Many school yards have traditional hopscotch boards on the pavement or you can draw one yourself with sidewalk chalk. Throw a stone into square one, hop over number one and then into every square up to number ten, back to number two and pick up the stone. Return to the beginning and throw to number two. You're out if you step outside the lines or in any squares that contain another player's stone.

Why not try a snail-shaped board? Use sidewalk chalk to draw a snail with a swirled shell and a head. Divide into ten steps with the head as one and the middle of the shell as ten. Play as regular hopscotch.

# ORDINARY, MOVINGS

Throw the ball against a wall while saying the instructions and doing the actions in brackets below. You must complete the action before catching the ball. If you get mixed up or drop the ball, start over or let another player have a turn.

If you complete all the actions in order, start over, this time wiggling your way through all the instructions, followed by smiling your way through and so on.

- ordinary (throw and catch the ball)

- movings (throw and catch the ball while wiggling around)

- laughing (smile)

- talking (put your finger over your mouth)

- one hand (catch the ball with one hand)

- the other hand (catch the ball with the other hand)

- one foot (stand on one foot)

- the other foot (stand on the other foot)

- clap front (clap both hands in front)

- clap back (clap hands behind your back)

- front and back (clap in front and then behind)

- back and front (clap behind and then in front)

- tweedles (twirl your hands around each other, away from your body)

- twydles (twirl your hands in the opposite direction)

- curtsies (curtsey)

- salutesies (salute)

- bowsies (bow)

- jumpsies (jump up and down)

- underground (bend one knee and clap both hands under it)

- away-you-go (spin around in a circle)

### RECESS REMEMBERED

In the old days, school yards were different. Names such as "the boys' track" or "the girls' hill" let kids know who could play where. Girls and boys even entered the school through separate doors. Teachers were allowed to spank children, using a leather belt called the strap. Ask if your grandparent ever got the strap for talking in line or fooling around with a friend.

There were bullies back then too. Ask your grandparent if he can still name the terror of the school yard.

# PENNY GAMES

**I**nvite your grandparents to play a game from their youth. All you need is a table and a few pennies.

## PENNY HOCKEY

**1.** One player makes the goal by pressing the knuckles of one hand against the side of the table and lifting pointer and baby fingers so they rest on the tabletop.

**2.** The other player, or forward, arranges three pennies in a triangle at the opposite end of the table, with one penny balanced over the edge of the tabletop.

**3.** The forward hits the penny (and edge of the tabletop) with the base of her palm so all three pennies shoot toward the goal.

**4.** The forward then shoots the penny that stops farthest from the goal so it slides between the other two pennies toward the goal. The shot is made by a flick of the finger so the fingernail hits the penny.

**5.** To be complete, the penny must pass between the other two pennies and land nearer the goal than either of the two pennies. If successful, the forward proceeds to step 6. If not, it is the opposing player's turn to be the forward.

**6.** Shots are repeated as in steps 4 and 5, until the forward shoots into the goal (one point). Then the players switch roles.

**7.** The player who scores the most goals wins the pennies.

# PENNY FOOTBALL

**1.** One penny is balanced on the edge of a tabletop and hit by the first player's palm.

**2.** The first player gets four "downs" (fingernail flick shots as in hockey) to move the penny so it stops overhanging the opposite tabletop edge. If unsuccessful, the player loses his turn and the opposing player starts at step 1.

**3.** When a player completes step 2, he flips the overhanging end of the penny up from underneath and catches it before it lands — all with the same hand. That is a touchdown (six points).

**4.** The opposing player makes a goal by forming two fists, pressing his knuckles together and lifting up his thumbs for goalposts.

**5.** The player who earned the touchdown now spins the coin on the table and stops it between his thumbs. He flicks it from between his thumbs, palms flat on the table, so the penny flies between the "goalposts" for the conversion (one point). The players switch roles and start again at step 1.

# FAMILY SKIT

Whe your family gathers to celebrate a grandparent's anniversary or birthday, provide the entertainment with a family skit. Write the script and produce the event, with a little help from your relatives. For a birthday celebration, the first step is to think about what makes your grandparent unique and special.

**1.** Review the life of your grandfather, for instance, decade by decade. Interview your parents, look at scrapbooks and family photos for ideas.

**2.** Choose a theme or a major accomplishment to represent every ten years. Include hobbies, sports, travels, career and special interests.

**3.** Does your grandfather have a trademark habit — such as wearing his glasses pushed up on his head while wondering where his glasses are? What are his pet peeves and favorite causes?

**4.** Write down a rough script and think of one or two props for each decade. Here's an example of how to celebrate the 70th birthday of a grandfather.

1930s: grows up poor in a big family (mock newspaper with The Depression as big headline)

1940s: becomes a bird-watcher (binoculars and field guide)

## THE PRODUCTION

- Choose a space to be your stage such as the garden, deck or living room. Place your props in a basket within reach of the stage.

- Ask a cousin or sibling to be your helper. He will act the part of your grandfather and can dress in one of his outfits.

- Using your script as a guide, tell a short and humorous history of your grandfather's life. At the beginning of each decade, give your helper a prop to put on or hold. By the end of the story, he will be staggering under the weight of your grandfather's life!

1950s: loves rock and roll (phonograph records, slicked-back hair)

1960s: gets married and starts a family (wedding ring and doll)

1970s: works hard in his career (briefcase)

1980s: takes up golf, still bird-watching (golf club)

1990s: becomes a grandfather (more dolls)

2000s: more golf, with grandson, teaches bird-watching (another golf club)

## PHOTO OPPORTUNITY

Have someone videotape or photograph your production. Then your grandparent can relive every moment.

# CRAFTS

**E**njoy making some tried and true crafts or

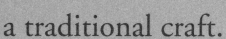

add your own flair to a traditional craft.

 Practice hand shadows and put on a show, create a pinball board and challenge your grandparent to a game, or, for a good laugh, 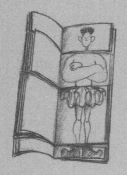 make a flip-page cartoon booklet. If you create and install a bird feeder together, you can sit back, relax and wait for your first feathered visitor.

# BEADING

**Y**our grandparent may remember daisy chains with real daisies, but this beaded daisy chain necklace will last forever. Make one for Grandma, Mom and your sister too.

### YOU'LL NEED

seed beads

a saucer or shallow dish

a beading needle

beading thread

scissors

**1.** Place the beads in a dish. You'll need green, white and yellow beads to make a traditional daisy chain, or use your favorite colors.

**2.** Thread the beading needle with about 1 m (3 ft.) of beading thread for a necklace, or 0.5 m (1½ ft.) for a bracelet. Double the thread and tie a knot at the end.

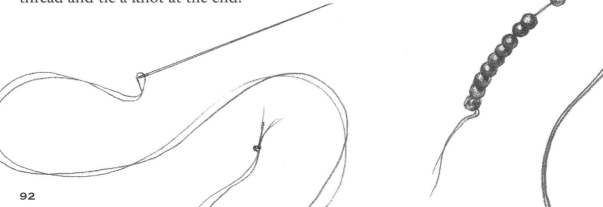

**3.** Thread on one green bead to the knot at the end of the thread. Pass the needle through the bead a second time to tie another knot.

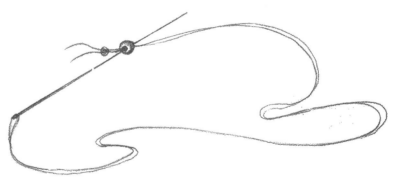

**4.** Thread on nine more green beads and pull to the knotted bead.

**5.** Thread on eight white beads. Holding the beads between your finger and thumb, pass the needle through the white beads again, pulling gently to form a loop.

**6.** Thread on one yellow bead and wedge it in the middle of the loop. Pass the needle through the fourth white bead and, holding the yellow bead in place, carefully pull the thread taut.

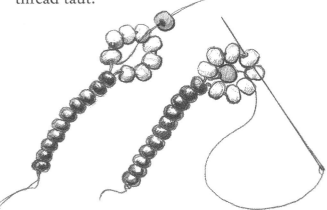

**7.** Thread on ten green beads.

**8.** Repeat this pattern until the necklace is the desired length.

**9.** To complete the chain, hold the beads until they form a closed circle. Pass the needle through the beginning of the necklace and work back through the pattern for approximately 10 cm (4 in.). Cut the thread close to the beads.

**Note:** If your thread gets short, reverse back through the last stem and flower and cut the thread. Thread the needle and tie a single knot. Pass through the last 5 cm (2 in.) of the necklace, hiding the knot inside the beads and continue your work.

# CAST-OFF TREASURES

Is there a button box or a costume jewelry box on your grandparent's dresser? Ask permission to sort through for interesting buttons or broken costume jewelry. Now create a recycled treasure by transforming an old button into a jazzy pin or hair clip.

# FAMILY STAMP

**C**ombine the old art of whittling with the newer craft of stamping. Carve a simple version of your family crest into an eraser and give it to your grandparents with an ink pad. They can print it onto such items as notepaper, envelopes, labels and books.

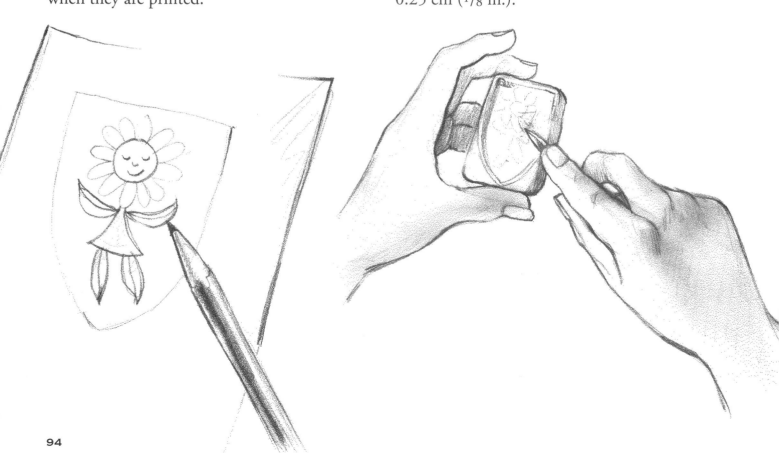

### YOU'LL NEED

a pencil

a large pink eraser

a sharp pocketknife or craft knife

an ink pad

paper

**1.** Draw a simple version of your family crest (see page 18) on the eraser. If you use letters or numbers on the design, you must draw them backward so that they will read forward when they are printed.

**2.** Carefully stroking the knife away from you, carve off the surface of the eraser around the outline of your design, right to the outside edges. Remove the surface to a depth of about 0.25 cm (1/8 in.).

**3.** With the point of your knife, carefully cut and dig out areas within the design that you do not want to show up when you print.

**4.** Test your stamp by pressing it on the ink pad and then onto paper. Carve off any unnecessary bits to improve the crest imprint.

## SIGNED, SEALED AND DELIVERED

Before the invention of good glues, people dripped warm wax from a lit candle on the edge of an envelope and then pressed a stamp on the wax to seal it. The stamp, originally called a seal, was often a carving of a family crest. If the wax was broken on the envelope, the receiver knew someone had been peeking inside. Waxed seals are still made for legal and ceremonial documents.

# PINBALL BOARD

**I**n your grandparents' time there were no video games, but kids played pinball at an arcade or made their own pinball boards. They played one another's boards and tried to earn the highest score for the board.

### YOU'LL NEED

a wooden board about
20 cm x 15 cm (8 in. x 6 in.)

a hammer

about 50 small nails

a felt-tipped marker

elastic bands

marbles

**1.** At the top left-hand corner of the board, hammer in 4 nails about 2.5 cm (1 in.) apart to form a square. Hammer the nails so they stand without wobbling, but do not break through the back of the board.

**2.** Stretch an elastic band between the 2 left nails and another between the 2 right nails. Write the word "start" inside the path between the elastics.

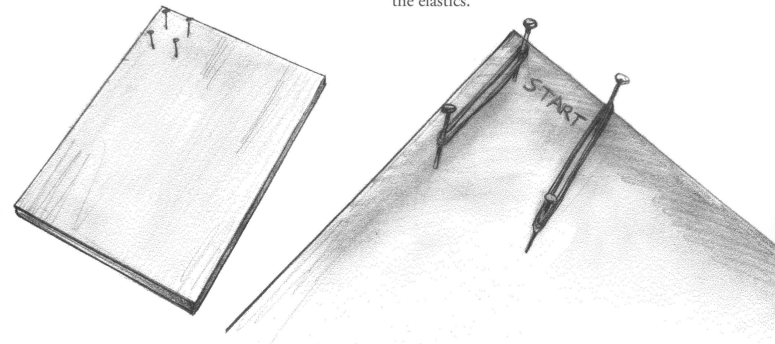

**3.** Repeat steps 1 and 2 for the top right-hand side of the board.

**4.** With 10 nails and 5 elastics, create four exit paths at the bottom of the board. With a marker, write the word "exit" in each of the paths as well as values, such as "win 1" or "lose 2."

**5.** Hammer nails in the middle of the board to form a maze. Stretch elastic bands between them. The nails and elastics are placed so that when the board rests on a slant and a marble is dropped at one of the starts, the marble keeps hitting nails and elastics until it exits through one of the bottom paths and scores.

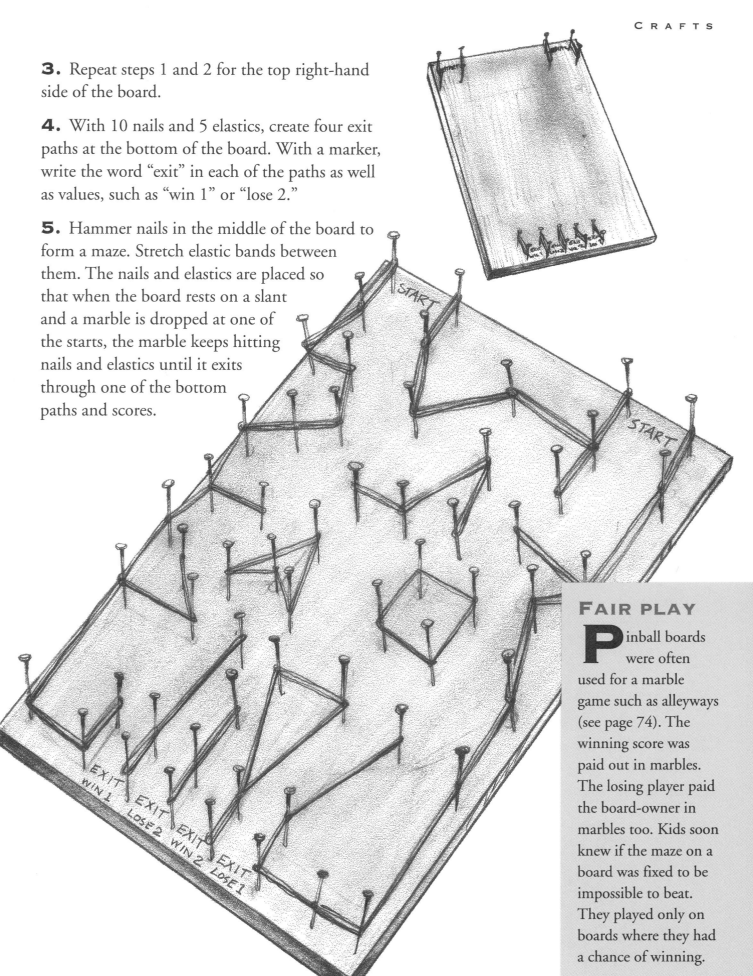

## FAIR PLAY

Pinball boards were often used for a marble game such as alleyways (see page 74). The winning score was paid out in marbles. The losing player paid the board-owner in marbles too. Kids soon knew if the maze on a board was fixed to be impossible to beat. They played only on boards where they had a chance of winning.

# WOOL CRAFTS

Ⅰf your grandparent has some leftover wool around, make these quick and easy tassels and pompoms together.

## TASSELS

Make tassels to finish off bookmarks, attach them to zippers, tie them to doorknobs, sneakers and ice skates, or add them to a wrapped parcel. Attach one to a piece of wool and dangle it under a cat's nose, and the chase is on!

| YOU'LL NEED |
| --- |
| heavy wool |
| a piece of cardboard, 10 cm x 10 cm (4 in. x 4 in.) |
| scissors |
| a darning needle |

**1.** Wrap wool snuggly around the middle of the cardboard about 50 times.

**2.** Cut three pieces of wool each 25 cm (10 in.) in length. Loop one piece under the middle of the wound wool. Knot it tightly.

**3.** Turn over the cardboard. Slide the scissors under the middle of the wool and cut.

**4.** Fold the wool in half with the knot in the middle. Tie a piece of wool around the fold close to the middle knot.

**5.** Thread the darning needle with a piece of wool and make a loop through the top of the tassel.

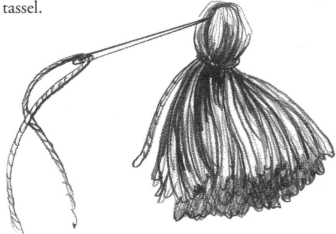

# POMPOM CRITTERS

Make pompoms with your grandparent and turn them into magnet critters.

**YOU'LL NEED**

thin wool

scissors

a piece of cardboard, 5 cm x 5 cm (2 in. x 2 in.)

a 10-cm (4-in.) piece of strong nylon string

construction paper

craft glue

wobbly eyes

magnetic strips

**1.** Wind the wool tightly around the cardboard at least 150 times.

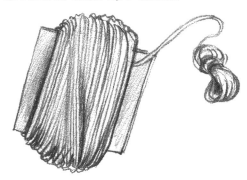

**2.** At one end, slide the nylon string between the wool and the cardboard. Tie it very tightly with three or four knots.

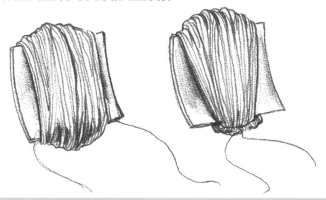

**3.** Bend and remove the cardboard. Cut the loops of wool and shake the pompom. Trim the wool into a ball.

**4.** Cut out a construction-paper base in the shape of feet and glue it to the bottom of the pompom. Glue on wobbly eyes.

**5.** Glue on a small magnetic strip and stick it to your grandparent's fridge.

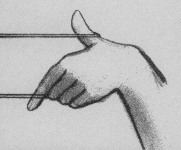

## STRING GAMES

**W**hile you're crafting pompoms, ask your grandparent if she remembers any string games such as cat's cradle.

# CANDLE MAKING

**I**f you have some candle stubs, you can make a new candle from them. Choose candle stubs of similar colors to melt together. If you don't have enough of one color, add white paraffin wax. Crayon will deepen the color.

### YOU'LL NEED

newspaper

a clean, dry 1 L (1 qt.) milk carton

scissors

a 20-cm (8-in.) candle

a small ball of Plasticine or other modeling material

a chopstick or long wooden spoon

candle stubs and old crayons

white paraffin wax (optional)

a potato peeler

a clean, empty coffee or juice can

an old double boiler or old pot

water

oil-based fragrance — lavender, pine, etc. (optional)

oven mitts

ice

**1.** Cover the table or counter with newspaper.

**2.** Trim the top of the milk carton with scissors, as shown.

**3.** Squeeze a ball of Plasticine onto the base of the candle. Center it in the bottom of the carton and push it firmly in place. If your fingers can't reach, use a chopstick or wooden spoon handle to push it in place.

**4.** Use the potato peeler to peel wax off the candle stubs. Discard the wicks.

**5.** Ask an adult to help you melt the wax. Half fill the can with wax shavings. Place the can in the pot.

**6.** Half fill the pot with warm water and place it on a back element of the stove. Turn on to low. The wax will take about 20 minutes to melt. As the wax melts, add more shavings. The melted wax should never more than half fill the can. It's best to melt the wax in batches.

**7.** Using a pot holder, remove the can from the pot and carry the melted wax to the table. At this point you can add a few drops of fragrance oil. Gently stir with a chopstick.

**8.** Carefully pour the melted wax into the carton. Avoid melting the candle inside by pouring down the sides. Continue adding melted wax until it reaches the wick of the candle.

**9.** If wax oozes out the seams of the carton, rub the carton with ice until the leak stops. When the wax is hard, rip off the carton.

## ROLLED CANDLES

Beeswax, once burned by cave people, is now available in colored sheets at craft stores. Cut one sheet in half, forming two triangles. Place the wick along the short edge of the triangle of one sheet. Lay the second sheet of wax beside the wick. Roll up the wax pieces tightly beginning from the wick side and you have a honey of a candle.

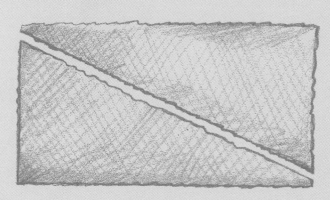

# STORYTELLER PUPPET

**R**etell your favorite family story with puppets. Make a storyteller puppet modeled after a family member. Choose that person's favorite colors and styles or ask your grandparents for a familiar brooch, tie or scarf to personalize the puppet even more.

### YOU'LL NEED

tempera paints

a paintbrush and jar of water

a large wooden spoon

scissors

thin cardboard

cloth

masking tape

an old sock

decoration materials such as buttons, yarn, beads, feathers and tinsel

white glue

## CRAFT SUPPLIES

**A**sk your grandparents where they got their craft supplies when they were kids. With few specialty stores, even white cardboard was hard to find — except from the packaging of men's shirts.

**1.** Paint your character's face on the back of the wooden spoon.

**2.** Cut a cardboard circle for a collar. Pierce a hole in the center and slide it along the spoon handle to the puppet's head.

**3.** Cut a cloth circle about 60 cm (24 in.) across. Cut a small hole in the center of the circle. Cut a 5-cm (2-in.) slit in the cloth about 15 cm (6 in.) from the center.

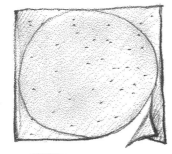

**4.** Slip the handle of the spoon through the center hole and up to the collar. Fasten the cloth to the spoon handle with masking tape.

**5.** Slip the toe end of the sock through the slit from the inside. Tape the sock onto the underside of the cloth so you can push three fingers through and move the sock as if it were the puppet's hand.

**6.** Glue on yarn for hair. Decorate the puppet's costume.

**7.** To work the puppet, one hand holds the spoon handle and the other moves the sock hand. Use the sock hand to add expression to your puppet's storytelling.

# CONE PUPPET

**C**one puppets were popular when your grandparents were little. You can make one and then keep younger family members laughing by playing peek-a-boo, using the puppet.

### YOU'LL NEED

white glue

a plastic-foam ball 5 cm (2 in.) across

a smooth stick or dowel narrow enough to push into the ball

scissors

a paper cup

a circle of fabric 30 cm (1 ft.) across

an elastic band

masking tape

decoration materials such as felt-tipped markers, wool, ribbon, felt, buttons and feathers

**1.** Dab glue on the tip of the stick and push it into the ball for a head.

**2.** Poke a small hole in the center of the cup bottom. Push the cup up the free end of the stick. The lip of the cup sits under the head.

**3.** Cut the circle of cloth in half and mark the centre point.

**4.** Drape the cloth around the stick so the center is just below the head. Fan the cloth into a skirt below the head and above the cup. Secure the cloth just below the head with an elastic band and pull some cloth above the elastic to form a collar.

**5.** Reduce the width of the skirt by overlapping the cloth to form a cone shape. Adjust it until the bottom of the cone of fabric meets the lip of the cup all around. Glue the bottom of the cone to the inside of the lip of the cup, or tape the fabric to the outside of the cup.

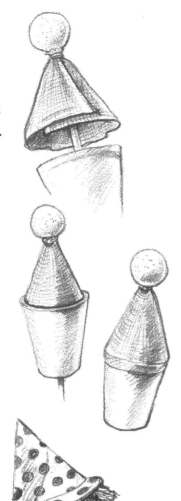

**6.** Decorate the head to make a face and add hair and a hat.

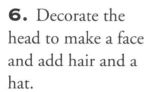

**7.** Hold the cup in one hand and slide the stick up and down with the other. The puppet's head peeks in and out of the cup.

# SPAGHETTI LEGS

Another old-fashioned puppet that children love is the wobbly person.

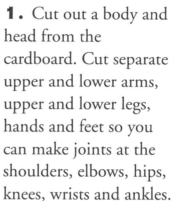

**YOU'LL NEED**

thin cardboard

scissors

a one-hole punch

paper fasteners

felt-tipped markers

**1.** Cut out a body and head from the cardboard. Cut separate upper and lower arms, upper and lower legs, hands and feet so you can make joints at the shoulders, elbows, hips, knees, wrists and ankles.

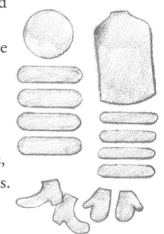

**2.** With the one-hole punch, make holes in each shoulder and hip, at each joint of the arms and legs and at the ankles and wrists.

**3.** Put the body together using paper fasteners. Draw on features with markers.

**4.** Hold the puppet's waist from the back and make it walk.

# HAND SHADOWS

**I**n old-fashioned movie theaters, kids in the audience would entertain themselves between reels with hand shadow shows. Ask your grandparents if they know any hand shadows. Set up a shadow theater by sitting beside a lamp pointed at a blank wall. A desk lamp with a clear bulb and an adjustable neck works best. Hold your hands between the light and the wall to perform.

## BUTTERFLY

Cross your hands at the wrists. Your fingers, held close together, form the wings. For the antennae, place your thumbs side by side, but not touching, in the middle. Gently move your fingers back and forth and fly across the wall. Bend one thumb down and the one remaining becomes the neck and head of a butterfly.

## ROOSTER

Slide your left hand around your right thumb. Your left thumb forms the lower half of the rooster's beak and the remaining fingers are the upper half of the beak. Wiggle the fingers of your right hand — that's the rooster's comb. When the rooster crows, open and shut your left hand.

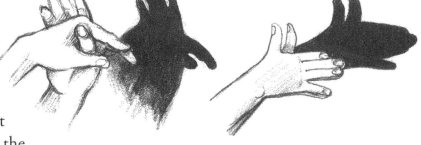

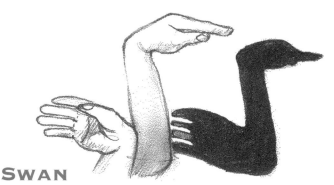

## SWAN

Bend your left arm with your forearm pointing up. Bend your left wrist, making your hand into the swan's head. Your fingers and thumb are the beak. Place the back of your right hand against the inside of your left elbow and open your fingers to form the back and tail of the swan.

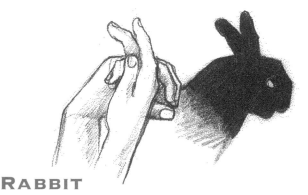

## RABBIT

Form an "O" with your left hand. Make a "V" with your right hand and place it beside the knuckles of your left hand. Wiggle the "V" — these are ears. Open and close the fingers of your left hand and your rabbit will appear to be nibbling on lettuce.

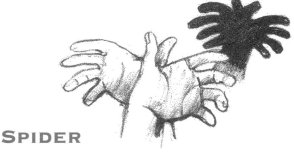

## SPIDER

Make the butterfly (page 106), but hook your thumbs together. Spread your fingers open and wiggle the eight legs of a very scary spider.

## DOG

Place your palms together as if to clap. Point your thumbs up and separate them, forming ears. Hold your middle three fingers together as the dog's snout. Move your little fingers up and down together to bark and snarl.

# NUTTY CRAFTS

Here are some old-time craft ideas that require neither kits nor shopping — just nature's freebees and odds and ends from around your grandparent's home.

## SLEEPY MOUSE BOOKMARK

With a few sewing leftovers, nuts and string, create this unique bookmark.

**YOU'LL NEED**

| |
| --- |
| ½ a walnut |
| a kitchen knife |
| a pistachio nut or a hazelnut |
| scissors |
| white glue |
| felt, lace, fabric and ribbon scraps |
| 20 cm (8 in.) string or thick wool |
| a thin black permanent marker |

**1.** With your grandparent's help, carefully clean out the walnut. Glue lace or ribbon to the edge of the walnut, if you like.

**2.** Glue the pistachio to one end of the walnut forming a mouse's head.

**3.** At the other end, glue the string, forming the mouse's tail.

**4.** Cut a piece of fabric or felt to cover the top of the walnut. Glue it in place, leaving the mouse's head and tail poking out.

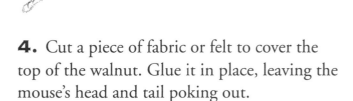

**5.** Cut out two small fabric ears and glue them on the pistachio nut. Draw on a face and whiskers.

# STRAWBERRY WALNUTS

Turn ordinary walnuts into strawberry ornaments. Add them to a bowl of fruit or hang them on a tree.

**YOU'LL NEED**

newspaper

12 walnuts

red and black tempera paint

a fine paintbrush

green ribbon, 0.5 cm (1/4 in.) wide

white glue

**1.** Protect your work area with newspaper. Paint the walnuts red and allow them to dry. Paint black dots on the red nuts and dry again.

**2.** For each walnut, cut a piece of ribbon 10 cm (4 in.) long. Fold it in half and glue it to the top of the walnut. Allow the glue to dry, before hanging the nuts.

# OLD-FASHIONED NUTTY FLAVORS

If you grow a giant vegetable (see page 118) or cut a jack-o-lantern, don't throw away the seeds. Roast them and experience a nutty taste from the past. Make sure you share them with your grandparents. Here's how:

- Rinse the pulp off the seeds and spread them on a dry cookie sheet. Dust with salt.

- Roast for 20 minutes at 150°C (300°F) or until crisp and brown.

- Remove from the oven with oven mitts and cool before eating.

# BIRDHOUSE

**Y**our grandparents may have noticed that there are fewer songbirds now than when they were kids. Towns and cities have grown so much that birds do not have as many places to nest. You can lure back cavity-nesting birds such as wrens by putting up a birdhouse in your grandparents' yard. Make this house together.

**YOU'LL NEED**

1.25 cm (1/2 in.) thick wood (pine is best)

a handsaw

white (carpenter's) glue

a hand drill with small (nail-sized) bit
and 2.5 cm (1 in.) bit

2.5 cm (1 in.) coated nails

a hammer

varnish

a paintbrush

eye screws or nails

wire (for hanging)

**1.** Ask an adult to help you precut your wood into pieces:

1 floor
6.25 cm x 6.25 cm
(2 1/2 in. x 2 1/2 in.)

1 lid
7.5 cm x 7.5 cm
(3 in. x 3 in.)

2 sides
7.5 cm x 15 cm
(3 in. x 6 in.)

1 back
6.25 cm x 15 cm
(2 1/2 in. x 6 in.)

1 front
8.75 cm x 15 cm
(3 1/2 in. x 6 in.)

1 hanging strip
2.5 cm x 25 cm
(1 in. x 10 in.)

**2.** Drill the entrance hole 2.5 cm (1 in.) wide in the front above the center point.

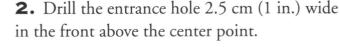

**3.** With the small bit, drill five air holes at the top of the back. Drill five more holes into the floor for drainage.

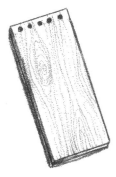

**4.** Assemble the box.

- At each stage, start nail holes with the drill and then hammer in nails to hold the pieces together.

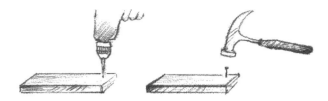

- Stand the back upright. Glue and nail one edge of the floor to the side of it.

- Glue, then nail, the sides against the assembled back and floor.

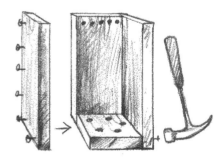

- From the inside of the box, nail the hanging strip down the outside of the back. Let it extend above and below the box and twist in an eye screw at each end.

- Nail the front against preglued edges of the sides and floor.

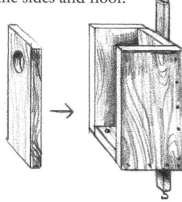

- Rub glue over the top edges of the box. Center and nail on the lid so it covers the top and overhangs the entrance.

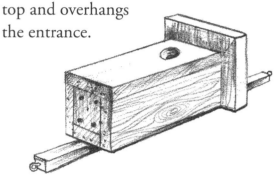

**5.** Varnish the house a natural brown color. Turn the page to find out how to hang your birdhouse.

# CHOOSING A SITE AND HANGING YOUR BIRDHOUSE

Wrens prefer to nest on the side of a tree or the top of a pole with shrubs nearby.

The entrance hole should be 2 m (6¹/₂ ft.) above the ground.

The entrance should face the sun for some of the day and away from the wind.

A squirrel or cat should not be able to jump from nearby shrubbery or branches to the nesting box.

A 60-cm (2-ft.) strip of metal or hard plastic wrapped tightly around the tree or pole below the box will keep cats and squirrels from climbing up from the ground.

If you hang the box on a tree, run lengths of wire through the top and bottom eye screws and around the tree, twisting the wires at the back of the tree until the box does not slip. To attach the box to a pole, hammer nails through the hanging strip where it extends above and below the box.

Do not place the box on a platform or attach a perch. These give enemies a foothold for stealing eggs and young birds.

Wrens prefer to nest where there are two boxes — one for their young and the other for spare twigs and grasses. Start to work on a second box.

# BIRD FEEDER

A ttract some birds and help them survive by providing food and shelter. Share this project with your grandparents and make one for your home and one for theirs.

## WINDOWSILL TRAY FEEDER

A simple tray feeder is perfect for apartments and where there are few squirrels.

| YOU'LL NEED |
| --- |
| 2 cm (3/4 in.) plywood or planks |
| a ruler |
| a pencil |
| a handsaw |
| a hammer |
| nails |
| two 30-cm (1-ft.) L brackets with screws |
| birdseed |

**1.** Choose a sheltered window close to trees or a balcony where birds can perch.

**2.** Cut a board a little longer than the length of the windowsill and 30 cm (1 ft.) wide.

**3.** Cut a strip of wood the length of the first board and 5 cm (2 in.) wide. Nail it to one edge of the board.

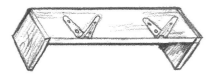

**4.** Cut two end pieces, 30 cm x 30 cm (1 ft. x 1 ft.) and nail them in place as shown.

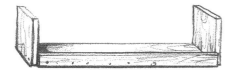

**5.** On the bottom of the feeder, screw L brackets 5 cm (2 in.) from each end.

**6.** With an adult's help, screw the L brackets into the wooden base of the windowsill.

**7.** Scatter birdseed on the tray, and wait for your first feathered visitor.

## LIFE LISTS

I f you and your grandparents become keen bird-watchers, keep a list of the different birds you have all seen. Many museums or nature clubs have lists of the birds living in your region. Check off your sightings on the list, starting with the birds attracted to your feeder.

# SIMPLE FEEDERS

You can attract birds to your grandparents' garden with a variety of foods. See how many types of birds find your menu appealing.

## PEANUT BUTTER CONES

Nut eaters big and small will snack from pinecones packed with peanut butter. Gather fallen pinecones, the kinds that have spaces in between their scales.

**1.** Tie a string loop at the top of each cone.

**2.** Using a small knife or your fingers smear crunchy peanut butter into all the nooks and crannies of the cones.

**3.** Roll the cones in some birdseed and hang them from tree branches.

## GRANDPA MURRAY'S LOG FEEDER

Many birds need fat in their winter diet.

**1.** Drill or chisel ten holes in a 50-cm (20-in.) log.

**2.** Screw a heavy-duty hook into the top of the log. Fill the holes with the mixture below and hang it outside.

**Log feeder recipe:**
50 mL (1/4 c.) peanut butter
50 mL (1/4 c.) lard or bacon dripping
50 mL (1/4 c.) cornmeal
50 mL (1/4 c.) birdseed

- Have an adult warm the peanut butter and lard on the stove until it's gooey.

- Stir in cornmeal and birdseed until the mixture is very stiff. Add extra birdseed if needed.

- Store in a plastic tub in the refrigerator.

# ORANGE NECTAR FEEDER

Attract hummingbirds, orioles and other nectar feeders using fresh citrus fruit.

**1.** With an adult's help, cut an orange in half and lay it flesh side down on a cutting board.

**2.** Poke a small hole in the orange's skin. Slide the orange onto a tree branch, or place orange halves on the tray of your windowsill tray feeder (see page 113).

# POPCORN GARLAND

You'll bring birds close to the house with a tasty garland wound around a tree. Use plain popcorn — stale or soggy popcorn works well.

**1.** Thread a fine needle with polyester thread and knot it at one end.

**2.** Gently push the needle through the middle of the popped kernel and pull it to the knot. Leave a little space between each piece of popcorn.

**3.** For extra nourishment, you can alternate fresh cranberries with the popcorn.

# AS GOOD AS WORMS

Do you ever worry what worm-eating birds, such as robins, can eat when a snowstorm covers the ground, locking in the worms? Come to the robins' rescue by sprinkling some raisins on a fence top or other flat surface. The raisins will help to keep the birds going until the snow melts.

# WINDOWSILL GARDENING

Y ou can grow a garden at your grandparents' home even if they have no backyard. A balcony or windowsill can produce a brave show of pansies or a feast of tomatoes.

Visit a garden center together and read the seed packages. Decide which plants will suit their place by considering these points:

- How sunny is the windowsill or balcony? On a south-facing ledge you can grow plants that like full sun. A north-face is best for shade plants.

- Windowsills and balconies are dry. Will you and your grandparents remember to water regularly — or should you look for seeds that like drier soil?

- How much space is available? Try to find seeds developed especially for container gardening such as dwarf or miniature varieties.

- What kind of container can you use? Your grandparents may want to use a special planter — or they may agree to tin cans or even plastic bags that are placed inside more attractive containers.

## PREPARING YOUR WINDOWSILL GARDEN

**1.** Make sure your container has small holes in the bottom so water can drain out.

**2.** Place the container on a saucer to catch the drips.

**3.** Place a layer of clean gravel in the bottom of the container.

**4.** Fill the container with soil. Read the seed package to find out the best kind to use. Consider buying sterilized soil as it will be free from the diseases that attack container plants.

## PLANTING

**1.** Soak the seeds in cool water for several hours before planting.

**2.** Plant the seeds to the depth suggested on the pack. Sprinkle the soil with water until a trickle shows on the saucer underneath.

**3.** Place the container on the windowsill. Water it whenever the surface of the soil becomes dry.

# FORCING BULBS

Brighten up your grandparents' winter with a show of springtime. If you plant tulip, daffodil or narcissus bulbs indoors in the fall, you can trick them into blooming early.

- Six weeks before you want flowers, place five or six bulbs on a shallow dish or pie-plate. You do not need drainage holes.

- Cover the bulbs — but not the shoot tips — with clean gravel.

- Cover the bottom of the dish with water and place it in a dark cupboard. Add water when the bottom of the dish looks dry.

- Once the shoots start to grow, bring your dish into daylight.

# GROWING A GIANT

**C**hallenge your grandparents to see who can grow the biggest vegetable. These instructions will help you to grow a giant pumpkin, but you can try growing a giant zucchini or squash with the same method.

a round-mouthed shovel

manure and compost

pumpkin seeds

garden clippers

**1.** Pumpkins grow best in a large, sunny space with rich soil. Find a garden of its own or the southern edge of a vegetable patch to grow your pumpkin.

**2.** Dig a hole about the size of a tire and 50 cm (20 in.) deep. Fill the hole with a mixture of 2/3 manure and 1/3 compost. Shovel soil on top, forming a mound. Prepare several mounds.

**3.** When the danger of frost is over in the spring, plant two or three seeds 1.5 cm (5/8 in.) deep in each mound.

**4.** Dampen the soil immediately after planting, but don't wash away the seeds. Water thoroughly in the early morning or late evening two or three times a week until harvest time in the fall.

**5.** Allow the plant to grow until it has covered the prepared area. Pinch off the ends of the vines to prevent the plant from taking over any surrounding garden.

**6.** After the plant flowers, small pumpkins form. Leave one or two to grow and snip off the rest. This will force the plant's energy into the vegetable.

**7.** Water and weed the pumpkin patch until late autumn or the first threat of frost. Cut it from the vine with clippers.

**8.** For the family records, weigh, measure and photograph your prize pumpkin.

# GRANDPA BILL'S SOUP

If you grow a pumpkin or squash small enough to fit in the oven, this soup, cooked right inside the vegetable, makes a spectacular meal.

**YOU'LL NEED**

| |
| --- |
| 1 medium pumpkin |
| 500 mL (2 c.) grated cheese |
| 500 mL (2 c.) French bread cut into large croutons |
| 500 mL (2 c.) milk |
| salt and pepper |
| oven mitts |
| a large plate |

**1.** Cut a lid out of the pumpkin and scoop out the pulp and seeds. (See page 109 if you want to toast the seeds.)

**2.** Fill the pumpkin 1/3 full with layers of bread and cheese.

**3.** Add milk to fill the pumpkin 2/3 full, as well as salt and pepper to taste.

**4.** Bake the pumpkin, with the lid on, at 175°C (325°F) for two to three hours until the skin turns a bronze color. Remove from the oven with oven mitts and place on a large plate.

**5.** Gently scrape the flesh from the inside of the pumpkin and stir in with the other ingredients. Ladle into bowls and enjoy.

# POTPOURRI

**S**hare this old-time craft with your grandparent and enjoy the sweet scent of summer, all year long.

## DRYING PETALS

Choose petals for drying from the flowers listed below — they will dry well and keep their color. Gather flowers on a dry summer afternoon. If you want to try other flowers, dry one blossom and if it works well, add it to the list. Check with an adult before picking any plants.

bachelor's button

delphinium

lavender

peony

carnation

dusty miller

lily

rose

cornflower

hydrangea

marigold

verbena

daffodil

iris

orange blossom

violet

**1.** Cover a large tray or cookie sheet with a piece of window screening or newspaper and spread the flowers out, leaving space between them.

**2.** Keep them in a room with well-circulated, dry air. Leave them undisturbed for at least ten days, until the petals are crisp and dry. Any moisture will spoil the potpourri.

**3.** Don't place them on a windowsill: the sun fades the color of the blooms.

**4.** When the flowers are dry, mix them together in a large bowl.

## SCENTING YOUR POTPOURRI

Letting your nose be your guide, add extra scent with about 5 mL (1 tsp.) of the following dried plants, spices or a few drops of essential oil. If you don't have any of the ingredients at home, you can buy them at health-food stores and bath shops.

**lavender** — a highly fragrant plant

**cedar shavings** — a woodsy smell

**pinecones or needles** — earthy and clean

**orange or lemon peel** — fresh, citrus scent

**spices** — cloves, nutmeg, cinnamon and allspice

**herbs** — rosemary, mint and sage

**essential oils** — rose, pine, lavender, orange and lemon verbena

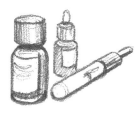

**orris root** — makes the scent of the potpourri last longer

# SACHETS

Wrap your homemade potpourri in cloth sachets. Then your grandparents can put the sachets in a drawer or sports bag and they'll have a pleasant reminder of you.

## YOU'LL NEED

2 pieces of cotton fabric, 15 cm x 10 cm (6 in. x 4 in.)

a needle and thread

an iron

ribbon

**1.** Fold the top 0.5 cm (1/4 in.) of the fabric to the inside of both pieces. Ask an adult to help you iron the fabric flat.

**2.** With right sides together, sew a 0.5 cm (1/4 in.) seam around the remaining three sides of the fabric. Turn right sides out and iron again.

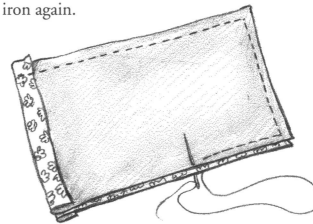

**3.** Half fill with potpourri and tie the open end shut with a piece of ribbon.

# FRUIT POMANDER

Make an old-fashioned natural air-freshener out of an orange. Studded with cloves, a pomander smells spicy and sweet.

**YOU'LL NEED**

fruit, such as an orange, apple or lemon
whole cloves
cinnamon, allspice and nutmeg
a small plastic bag
ribbon

**1.** Push the stems of cloves into the skin of the fruit, covering the entire surface.

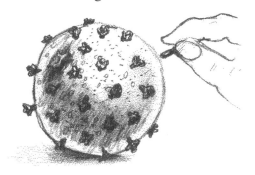

**2.** Measure 15 mL (1 tbsp.) each of cinnamon, allspice and nutmeg into a small plastic bag. Drop in the fruit. Twist the top of the bag shut and gently shake the bag, covering the fruit with a dusting of spices.

**3.** Wrap a piece of ribbon around the fruit and knot on top. Wrap a second piece of ribbon around the fruit, criss-crossing the first one, and tie a bow on top.

**4.** Attach a piece of ribbon to the bow and hang in a closet, from a chandelier or on a doorknob. The fruit will dry and shrink in size, but the fragrance will last for months.

# PRESSING FLOWERS

Your grandparents may have pressed flowers and leaves when they were young. Many grandparents still carry four-leafed clovers pressed in their wallets or between the pages of a book. Four-leafed clovers are uncommon and are considered good luck charms. You'll find that all kinds of pressed flowers and leaves add a charming, old-fashioned touch to your craft making.

## MAKING A FLOWER PRESS

### YOU'LL NEED

2 pieces of corrugated box cardboard, each about 30 cm x 45 cm (12 in. x 18 in.)

a kitchen knife

2 pieces of ribbon, 1 cm (1/2 in.) wide, or 2 bootlaces, each 1 m (3 ft.) long

10 or more newspaper sheets

**1.** Carefully poke small slits in both pieces of cardboard as shown.

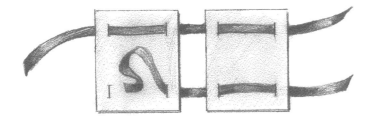

**2.** Weave the ribbons through the slits to make a book.

**3.** Fold about ten sheets of newspaper separately so each sheet is folded to the size of the cardboard pieces.

**4.** Place the folded newspaper sheets inside the cardboard. Pull the ribbons together tightly and tie the ends in a bow.

**5.** Take the press with you as you pick flowers and leaves. Open the press and lay your cuttings on the newspaper sheets, arranged as you want them once they dry. Plants of equal thickness should be pressed together on one sheet.

**6.** Tie the ribbons together so the pressing starts immediately.

**7.** Once home, add more newspaper throughout to blot up moisture. Retie the press and cover it with heavy books.

**8.** For the best color, do not disturb for at least three weeks.

## COLLECTING PLANTS TO PRESS

- Be sure you have permission to cut plants.

- Take only the flower, stem and one or two leaves with one snip of the scissors. Do not disturb the roots.

- Collect plants in mid-morning to mid-afternoon on dry days.

- Collect only common garden flowers or wildflowers, leaves and ferns. Thin, nonfleshy plants press best.

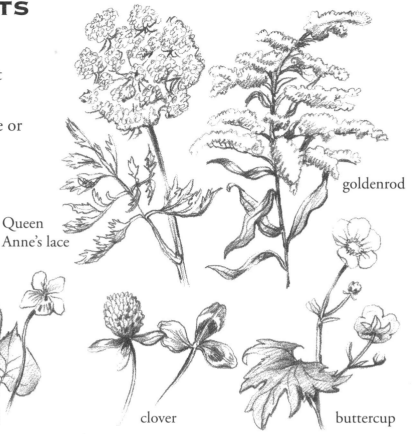

goldenrod

Queen Anne's lace

violet

clover

buttercup

## USING PRESSED FLOWERS

Pressed flowers are an elegant addition to paper decorations. Use them to make place cards for the family dinner table, invitations, greeting cards or bookmarks. Attach your dried plants to the prepared card or paper using white glue and a toothpick. Then protect your final product with clear, self-adhesive plastic.

# WAXED LEAVES AND DRIED FLOWERS

**Y**ears ago, people dried flowers and waxed leaves to keep the colors of summer and autumn glowing in their homes through dull winters. Today we can buy fresh flowers and plants year round. However, an old-fashioned waxed and dried arrangement still has an advantage — it needs no watering!

## DRYING FLOWERS

Flowers and plants that press well (see page 125) can also be dried whole and still keep their natural colors. There are others that only dry well whole.

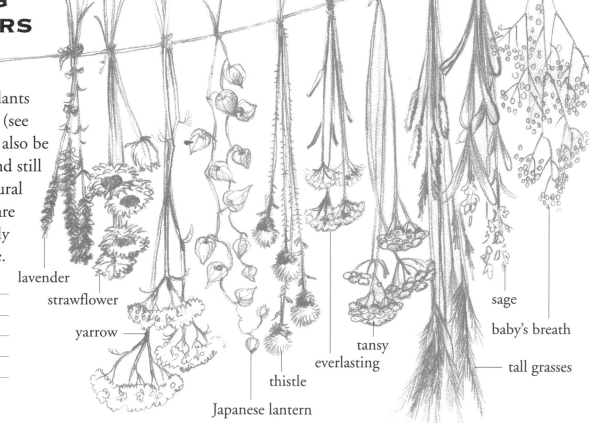

lavender
strawflower
yarrow
Japanese lantern
thistle
everlasting
tansy
sage
baby's breath
tall grasses

### YOU'LL NEED

scissors

twist ties

clothespins

a clothesline or coat hanger in a dark, dry room

**1.** Ask permission before you pick garden plants.

**2.** Collect plants on dry mornings before they wilt in the sun. Snip the stems carefully — the longer the stem, the better. Don't disturb the roots.

**3.** Remove all leaves from the stem.

**4.** Tie three or four flowers together at the base of the stems with a twist tie.

**5.** Hang in bunches upside down over the clothesline or coat hanger. Secure the flowers with clothespins.

**6.** Allow them to dry for at least a week before using them in an arrangement.

# WAXING LEAVES

When leaves dry, they usually curl, fade and then crumble to pieces. You can preserve their beautiful shapes and colors by waxing them. Collect leaves for waxing in the peak of their autumn color.

**YOU'LL NEED**

an iron

waxed paper

clean cotton rags

a small branch or individual leaves

scissors

**1.** Ask an adult to help you with the ironing in this activity.

**2.** Place a clean rag on your ironing surface and a piece of waxed paper on the rag.

**3.** Lay the leaves on the waxed paper and put individual pieces of waxed paper on top of each leaf.

**4.** Place a corner of another rag over one leaf at a time and iron the rag on low heat until it feels warm, not hot. The wax on the paper underneath should melt onto the leaves.

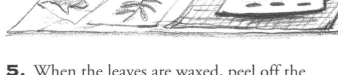

**5.** When the leaves are waxed, peel off the waxed paper and spread the leaves out to cool.

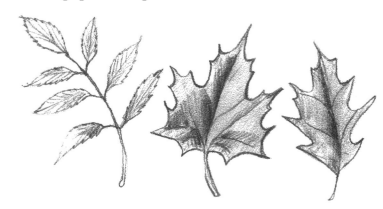

# MAKING ARRANGEMENTS

Use your waxed leaves and dried flowers in arrangements for display in vases or entwined into wreaths. They make great centerpieces for the family dinner table. Sprinkle the tablecloth around the centerpiece with leftover leaves and flower heads.

# MIX 'N MATCH BOOKS

**W**hen your grandparents were kids, people or animal mix-and-match booklets were popular. These little books were made with the pages cut into sections, one for the head, one for the body and one for the tail or feet. The reader flipped the sections to make crazy creatures.

## YOU'LL NEED

| |
| --- |
| 10 pieces of thin cardboard, 12 cm x 30 cm (4$\frac{1}{2}$ in. x 1 ft.) |
| a ruler |
| a pencil |
| a stapler |
| scissors |

**1.** Measure and draw a light pencil line down the length of nine of the pieces of cardboard, 1 cm ($\frac{1}{2}$ in.) from the left side. Fold along the pencil line and work the fold back and forth so the cards bend both ways.

**2.** Staple the nine cards together to make a booklet.

**3.** Sketch the outline of a person's body on the tenth card. Use as much of the card as you can except the left-hand edge. Cut the shape out to make a stencil.

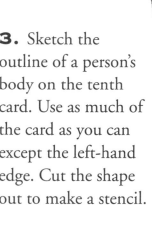

**4.** Center the stencil on the front page of the booklet, to the right of the fold, and trace around it lightly with your pencil.

**5.** Take measurements so you know how far up from the bottom and in from the right side you placed the stencil on the card.

**6.** Using these measurements as a guide to placing the stencil, repeat step 4 for the remaining pages of the booklet.

**7.** Using the outlines to guide you, draw and color one person on each page. Some can be girls, some boys and each should wear a different outfit, hairdo and shoes. Search through family photo albums for ideas. Talk to your grandparents, who may remember some outrageous or elegant styles to include.

**8.** On the first page of the booklet, draw lines with a pencil and a ruler across the card at the base of the neck, waist and ankles. Cut along these lines from the right side to the fold on every page of the booklet except the last page. Now flip the sections to mix and match the drawings.

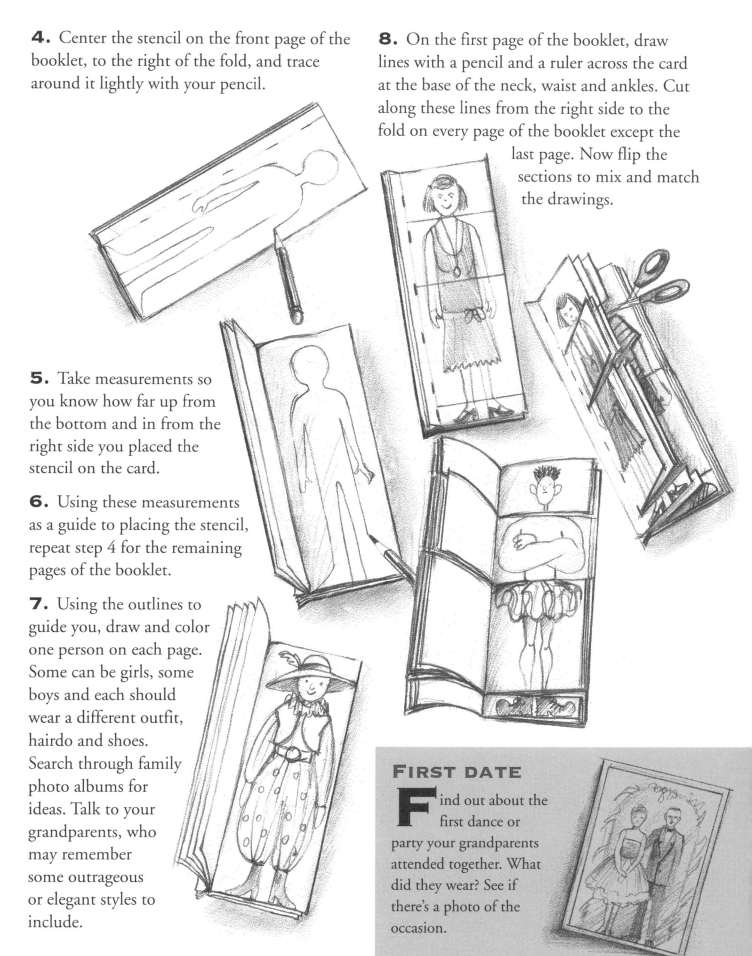

## FIRST DATE

**F**ind out about the first dance or party your grandparents attended together. What did they wear? See if there's a photo of the occasion.

129

# ANIMATED CARTOON

**Y**our grandparents may remember the first movie-length cartoons. Everyone was amazed because they knew cartoonists have to draw thousands of nearly identical pictures to make the characters seem to move. However, cartoonists do have some tricks to cut back on their work. Follow these directions and you can easily make a 50-page animated cartoon.

**YOU'LL NEED**

a pencil

a piece of thin cardboard, about 8 cm x 8 cm (3 in. x 3 in.)

felt-tipped markers, including black

a 50-page notepad or a pad of sticky notes, about 8 cm x 8 cm (3 in. x 3 in.)

**1.** Choose a simple cartoon character like a fish or a bumblebee. Draw an outline of your character on the cardboard so its nose is facing right.

**2.** Draw over the outline with black marker. Add the eye, fins, wings, stripes or other important features with marker. This is the stencil of your character.

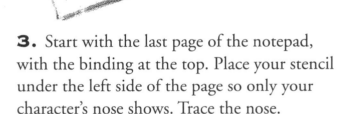

**3.** Start with the last page of the notepad, with the binding at the top. Place your stencil under the left side of the page so only your character's nose shows. Trace the nose.

**4.** Move to the second last page. Place the stencil under it, but the width of two pencil lines more to the right. Trace what you see. Continue through the notepad so that each time the character moves two pencil lines to the right. When you are showing the entire character, you can make small changes to the fins or the wings to suggest movement.

**5.** As you finish at the top page, the character will have moved so far right that all you will see is the tail leaving the page.

**6.** Go back over all your tracings with marker and add color if you like.

**7.** Now, flip the pages, back to front, and watch your character move.

## SHALL WE DANCE?

Ask your grandparents to show you one of the dances from their younger days—the jive, the jitterbug or the twist. Try to make a cartoon booklet of the dance step. You'll have to make several stencils—one of a figure at the starting position and a couple more at other positions of the step. Then alternate the stencils as you trace through your flip-page cartoon booklet.

# GIFT GIVING

**H**ere are some ideas for wrapping and presenting your homemade crafts to give as gifts to your grandparents.

## GIFT BOXES

You can make boxes from greeting cards, paper-backed metallic foil and wrapping paper. Fold one box slightly larger than another to make a lid.

**YOU'LL NEED**

thin, white cardboard

scissors

a ruler

**1.** Cut the cardboard in a 15 cm x 15 cm (6 in. x 6 in.) square. Trim to make sure the side measurements are exact and the angles are square.

**2.** Follow the diagram instructions using this symbol key:

**fold** — the arrow shows the direction of the fold

**crease** — a line made on the paper by making a fold and opening it up again

**pull** — fingers show direction to open the box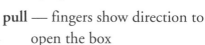

**3.** Fold, crease and pull the cardboard, working in the numbered order. Place each fold carefully with corners matching and edges meeting. Rub a fingernail along every fold so the fold line is clean and sharp.

1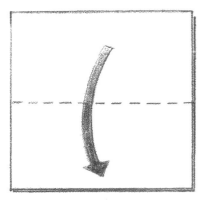

2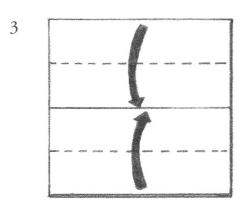

3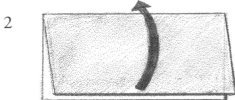

4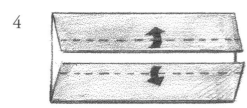

5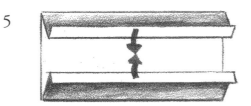

6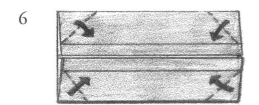

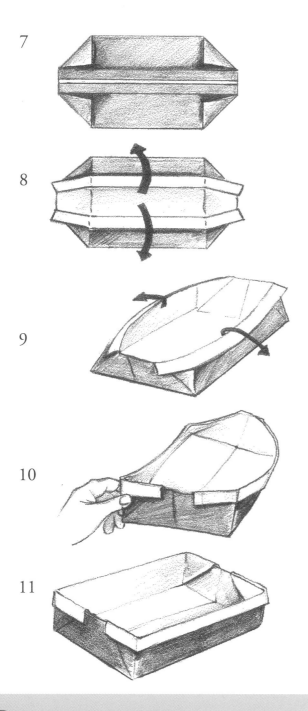

7

8

9

10

11

## BOXES IN BOXES

Once you are good at making boxes, try making a series, each slightly larger than the previous one, and place them inside one another. With lids for each, you will have made an old-fashioned toy — a gift in itself. Or you can put a tiny gift in the smallest box.

# GIFT BAG

You can make a gift bag that will last several givings if you use sturdy, art-quality paper. Decorate the paper before you turn it into a gift bag.

**YOU'LL NEED**
an old lunch bag
decorated paper
a pencil
scissors
white glue
wool

**1.** Carefully pull apart the glued seams of your lunch bag. Lay it open on a table and flatten the paper with your hands. This is your pattern to make a gift bag.

**2.** Lay the good side of your decorated paper facedown with the pattern on top. Using a pencil, trace the pattern onto your decorated paper. Cut along the traced lines and wherever else the pattern is cut.

**3.** Fold your decorated paper wherever your lunch bag pattern is folded.

**4.** Using the folds, form your gift bag and glue where the lunch bag is glued.

**5.** Cut two wool handles, each about 25 cm (10 in.). Poke two slits through the top of each side of the bag and thread through the wool. Knot the ends from the inside.

# FAMILY FOOD

The aroma wafting up from the kitchen hits your nose and says "dinner is ready." Taste buds go on alert and by the first bite you know it's grandmother's mouth-watering lasagna.

Foods shared with family can be more than just nourishment.  You'll never forget the taste of Grandpop's cookie surprise.

And, everyone craves Grandma Donna's ultra-rich chocolate cake, every single birthday. Try these family-style recipes for food and feasting with your grandparents. As you cook and clean up together, you'll discover the ingredients for great stories too. Remember to ask for an adult's help using knives, the stove or other appliances.

# SWEET-TOOTH FUDGE

**H**ere is a recipe for uncooked fudge that is rich and chocolatey. Make some with your grandparents and see if they have any sweet recipe ideas.

### YOU'LL NEED

1 egg

45 mL (3 tbsp.) heavy cream or condensed milk

10 mL (2 tsp.) vanilla

300 mL (1 1/4 c.) icing sugar

a pinch of salt

350 g (12 oz.) bag semisweet chocolate chips

15 mL (1 tbsp.) butter

300 mL (1 1/4 c.) miniature marshmallows or walnut pieces or crispy rice cereal (optional)

a mixing bowl

an electric mixer or hand mixer

a heavy-bottomed pot or a microwave-safe bowl

an oven mitt

a wooden spoon

waxed paper

a pan, 20 cm x 20 cm (8 in. x 8 in.)

a knife

plastic wrap

**1.** In the mixing bowl, combine the egg, cream, vanilla, icing sugar and salt. Beat together with your mixer until well blended.

**2.** Put on the oven mitt and melt the chocolate and butter in the pot over low heat on the stove. Stir with the wooden spoon until melted. If you have a microwave, put the chocolate and butter in a microwave-safe bowl and microwave for two minutes on high, or until melted.

**3.** After the chocolate has cooled down a little, add it to the egg mixture and beat with a mixer until smooth and creamy.

## PENNY CANDY

**H**ow many blackballs can you buy for a penny? Blackballs were three for a penny when your grandparents were kids. For ten dollars you could get a wagonload. Do your grandparents have any penny candy stories?

**4.** Stir in the marshmallows, crispy rice cereal or walnut pieces with the wooden spoon.

**5.** Cover the inside of your pan with waxed paper. Pour the mixture into the pan and smooth the top with the wooden spoon.

**6.** Refrigerate for at least one hour. Cut it into squares and store covered with plastic wrap in the refrigerator.

# THE COOKIE JAR

**S**tock up the cookie jar with these old favorites. Is there a secret family recipe you can learn from your grandparents?

## GRANDMA MARY ELLEN'S GINGER COOKIES

Roll and cut out this dough with cutters, or drop by the spoonful and cook into tantalizing mounds.

**YOU'LL NEED**

| |
|---|
| 175 mL (3/4 c.) soft margarine or butter |
| 250 mL (1 c.) white sugar |
| 1 egg |
| 50 mL (1/4 c.) molasses |
| 625 mL (2 1/2 c.) of flour |
| 5 mL (1 tsp.) salt |
| 5 mL (1 tsp.) baking soda |
| 5 mL (1 tsp.) cinnamon |
| 5 mL (1 tsp.) cloves (optional) |
| 15 mL (1 tbsp.) ground ginger |
| waxed paper |
| a rolling pin |
| cookie cutters (optional) |
| a spatula |
| a cookie sheet |
| oven mitts |
| a hot pad |

**1.** Preheat the oven to 180°C (350°F).

**2.** Combine sugar and margarine. Add egg and molasses and mix until smooth.

**3.** Set aside 125 mL (1/2 c.) of flour. Mix the remaining ingredients in a small bowl. Gradually add to the above mixture and stir into a stiff dough.

**4.** Divide the dough into three balls, place in a bowl and cover with waxed paper. Refrigerate for 20 minutes.

**5.** Dust the counter and rolling pin with some of the reserved flour. Roll out a ball of dough until it's 0.25 cm (1/8 in.) thick. Roll the dough out from the center. Do not turn the dough over. Add more flour if it becomes sticky.

**6.** Cut with cookie cutters or with a cup. Lift 12 cookies onto an ungreased cookie sheet with a spatula. Leave spaces for the cookies to swell as they cook.

**7.** Bake for 12 minutes. Remove from the oven with oven mitts and cool on a hot pad for one minute. With a spatula, lift from the pan onto a tray. Cool completely before placing in a cookie jar.

**8.** Repeat steps 5 through 7 with the other dough balls. Gather any leftover dough and form it into a final ball. Roll out again or form small circles with your hands before cooking.

# GRANDPOP'S COOKIE SURPRISE

These cookies on a stick are delicious plain or with a hidden chocolate surprise inside.

| YOU'LL NEED |
| --- |
| 50 mL (1/4 c.) margarine |
| 125 mL (1/2 c.) sugar |
| 1 egg |
| 5 mL (1 tsp.) vanilla |
| 2 mL (1/2 tsp.) baking powder |
| a pinch of salt |
| 300 mL (1 1/4 c.) white flour |
| chocolate chips (optional) |
| sprinkles (optional) |
| waxed paper |
| Popsicle sticks |
| oven mitts |
| a cookie sheet |

**1.** Preheat the oven to 180°C (350°F).

**2.** Combine the margarine and sugar. Add the egg and vanilla and stir until smooth.

**3.** Stir in the baking powder and salt. Gradually add the flour and beat into a stiff dough.

**4.** Cover the dough with waxed paper and refrigerate for 15 minutes.

**5.** Take a heaping teaspoon of dough and form a flat circle. Place on the cookie sheet. For a hidden chocolate surprise, put four to six chocolate chips on top.

**6.** Place a Popsicle stick on each cookie. Cover with another circle of dough, pinching the edges together. Scatter the cookie tops with a few sprinkles.

**7.** Bake for 10 to 12 minutes, until golden. Remove from the oven using oven mitts. Cool for a minute before removing from the pan.

# ROCKY ROAD SQUARES

Marshmallows or soft gummy candies, peanuts and chocolate cooked together make this sweet and sticky treat.

**YOU'LL NEED**

| |
|---|
| 350 g (12 oz.) chocolate chips |
| 1 can (14 oz) sweetened condensed milk |
| 25 mL (2 tbsp.) margarine |
| 500 mL (2 c.) chopped peanuts |
| 10 oz. miniature marshmallows or soft gummy candies |
| a medium-sized, heavy saucepan |
| a large mixing bowl |
| a pan, 33 cm x 23 cm x 5 cm (13 in. x 9 in. x 2 inc.) |
| waxed paper |

**1.** Line the pan with waxed paper.

**2.** In a pot, combine chocolate chips, condensed milk and margarine and stir over a low heat. Remove from the heat when melted.

**3.** Combine peanuts and marshmallows in a large bowl. Add the chocolate mixture and stir well.

**4.** Pour into the prepared pan and refrigerate for two hours. Cut and serve.

## WHO STOLE THE COOKIE?

**W**hile you're waiting for the cookies to bake, sing and clap this old chant. Say the words with the emphasis on the capitalized words, using your family names.

WHO stole the COOKIES from the COOKIE jar? Was it YOU, GRANDDAD? Who ME? YES you. COULDN'T BE. THEN who? GREGORY stole the COOKIES from the COOKIE jar. Who ME? YES you. COULDN'T BE…

# FAMILY BIRTHDAY CAKE

**G**randma Donna's deluxe chocolate birthday cake is so rich and delicious, you and your family might want it on every occasion.

## YOU'LL NEED

125 mL (1/2 c.) soft margarine or butter

500 mL (2 c.) white sugar

2 eggs

500 mL (2 c.) white flour

125 mL (1/2 c.) cocoa

2 mL (1/2 tsp.) salt

5 mL (1 tsp.) baking powder

5 mL (1 tsp.) baking soda

175 mL (3/4 c.) milk

5 mL (1 tsp.) vinegar

5 mL (1 tsp.) vanilla

175 mL (3/4 c.) boiling water

mixing bowls

an electric mixer

a sifter or fine sieve

a spoon

a spatula

a large cake tin 33 cm x 23 cm x 27 cm (13 in. x 9 in. x 11 in.)

**1.** Preheat the oven to 170°C (325°F).

**2.** In a large bowl, combine margarine, sugar and eggs and beat with the mixer until creamy and smooth.

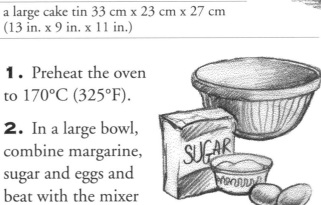

**3.** Sift the flour, cocoa, salt, baking powder and soda into a medium bowl. Re-sift three times.

**4.** In a small bowl, combine milk, vinegar and vanilla.

**5.** Add the flour and milk mixtures, a little at a time, to the large bowl. Beat well, scraping down the sides of the bowl with a spatula.

**6.** Slowly blend in the boiling water.

**7.** Grease the pan with a little margarine. Pour the batter into the pan, scraping out the bowl with the spatula.

**8.** Bake for 40 minutes. To test if the cake is cooked, gently press a finger into the middle of it. If the cake springs back up, it is done. Cool for a few minutes before removing from the pan. Cool to room temperature before icing.

## THE ICING

**YOU'LL NEED**

3 squares unsweetened chocolate

125 mL (¹/₂ c.) margarine

375 mL (1¹/₂ c.) icing sugar

5 mL (1 tsp.) vanilla

25 mL (2 tbsp.) boiling water

1 egg

**1.** Melt the chocolate and margarine together (see page 136, step 2).

**2.** Beat in the icing sugar, vanilla, boiling water and egg.

**3.** Spread generously on the top and sides of the cake.

## BIRTHDAY BONUS

In some families, it's a tradition to hide money in a birthday cake. Make sure everyone knows there are coins hidden inside. Use a variety of coins but only one dollar coin. Will the birthday guest of honor get the big coin?

**1.** Boil the coins for ten minutes in salted water. Cool.

**2.** Wrap each coin in a small piece of waxed paper.

**3.** Cut slits in the cake where you think the slices will be. Slip in the wrapped coins.

**4.** Cover the cake with a thick coating of icing.

# FUN FOOD TO SHARE

H ere's your chance to cook for your grandparents, and introduce them to one of these fun recipes.

## NO FUSS PIZZA

**YOU'LL NEED**

at least one English muffin per person

tomato sauce

mozzarella cheese, thinly sliced

precooked bacon bits, pepperoni or vegetable toppings

a cookie sheet

oven mitts

**1.** Have an adult preheat the oven to broil.

**2.** Slice the English muffins in half and place on a cookie sheet.

**3.** Spread 15 mL (1 tbsp.) tomato sauce on each half. Top with mozzarella cheese and meat or vegetables.

**4.** Broil for approximately one minute or until the cheese is melted. Use oven mitts to carefully remove from the oven. Cool slightly before eating.

## HOME DELIVERY

"W hat will we order tonight? Pizza, wings or Chinese food?" These words were never spoken in your great grandparents' homes. When they were kids there was no pizza delivery, meals were homemade. Basic essentials, such as bread, milk and coal were delivered by cart and horse or truck. The ice wagon brought ice for early refrigerators.

# PERFECT GRILLED CHEESE

**1.** For each sandwich, spread margarine on two slices of bread.

**2.** Cover one slice of bread on the dry side with cheese. Place the second slice of bread over the cheese, margarine-side up.

**YOU'LL NEED**

2 slices of bread per sandwich

margarine

marble or mozzarella cheese, thinly sliced

pickles

ketchup

a frying pan

a spatula

oven mitts

Note: Use low fat cheese and a small quantity of margarine for a healthier sandwich.

**3.** Warm the frying pan over a medium heat. Slide a spatula under the sandwich and place it, margarine-side down, into the frying pan. Cook for about one minute per side, until toastie brown.

**4.** Remove from the pan and cool slightly. Cut in half and enjoy with pickles and ketchup.

# PICK YOUR OWN

It's fun to go into the countryside to pick fruits and vegetables. Check the local paper for "pick-your-own" farms or orchards and plan an outing with your grandparents. If you pick a peck or a bushel, you'll have to do something with your harvest. That calls for a day of preserving, "putting down" or canning.

## TWO-FISTED PICKING

Whether you are picking berries from a bush or apples from a tree, it's best to have both hands free. Then you can reach for the choicest fruit without spilling what you've already picked. All you need is a 4- or 6-qt. basket and a piece of cord 50 cm (20 in.) bigger than your waist measurement. Knot the cord around the handle of the basket and then tie it around your waist. Now, pop a berry in your mouth and get picking.

## PICKING ATTIRE

Successful harvesting is closely linked to the weather. Some foods such as strawberries can spoil if picked wet. Plants such as beans may die if handled after a rain. It's best to go out picking on a clear summer's day — blue sky, sunshine and a bit of a breeze. Many berry bushes have thorns and some vegetable plants, like zucchini, are spiny and irritate the skin. On those occasions, wear lightweight long-sleeved clothes. Don't forget a broad-brimmed hat, sunscreen and a cool drink.

# GRANDMA FRAN'S DILLED BEAN STICKS

If you like store-bought cucumber pickles, you'll love these yellow bean pickles. But, you'll have to wait a month before you eat them.

**YOU'LL NEED**

| |
|---|
| 1.36 kg (3 lb.) young yellow beans (4-qt. basket) |
| sterile mason jars |
| 250 mL (1 c.) chopped fresh dill |
| 2 cloves garlic, peeled and quartered |
| 500 mL (2 c.) water |
| 500 mL (2 c.) white vinegar |
| 50 mL (1/4 c.) pickling salt |
| 20 mL (4 tsp.) sugar |
| 2 mL (1/2 tsp.) cayenne pepper |

**1.** Thoroughly wash the beans. Trim both ends of each bean.

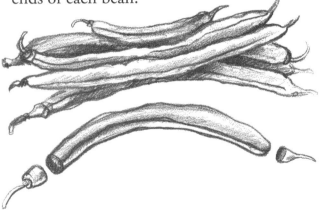

**2.** With an adult's help, cook the beans in boiling salted water for eight to ten minutes, until crisp but tender.

**3.** Drain and place in a sink of ice water for several minutes to stop the cooking and quickly cool the beans. Drain again and pat dry with a clean cloth.

**4.** Snuggly pack the beans upright in the jars. The beans should not be squished.

**5.** Divide the dill and garlic among the jars.

**6.** Heat the remaining ingredients and pour into the jars. Seal and store in the refrigerator for one month before eating.

# GRANDPA JOE'S APPLESAUCE

Preserve the flavor of an autumn day by making applesauce. It can be your contribution to the family feasts at Thanksgiving or Christmas.

### YOU'LL NEED

20 small apples (melba, spy or other white, firm fleshed apples)

a vegetable peeler

a cutting board

a paring knife

a large pot with a lid

375 mL (1 1/2 c.) of water

salt

a potato masher

oven mitts

a sieve

a large bowl

125 mL (1/2 c.) honey or white sugar (optional)

cinnamon

clean margarine tubs with lids or jars

**1.** Thoroughly wash the apples. Peel, slice into quarters and cut out the core. Thinly slice into a large pot.
Hint: Slice the apples into a bowl of salted water to keep them from turning brown as you work.

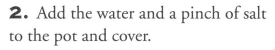

**2.** Add the water and a pinch of salt to the pot and cover.

**3.** Bring the water to a boil over medium-high heat. Remove the lid and turn the heat to low. Simmer for about 20 minutes,

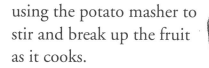

using the potato masher to stir and break up the fruit as it cooks.

**4.** Remove the pot from the stove, using oven mitts. Place the sieve in a large bowl and pass the applesauce through the sieve about 250 mL (1 c.) at a time. Add a pinch of cinnamon.

**5.** Taste the applesauce. If it's sour, return the applesauce to the pot and add sugar or honey. Dissolve the sugar by heating again, stirring constantly, for about one minute. Remove from the heat and cool.

**6.** Ladle into margarine tubs or jars, put on the lids, label and freeze.

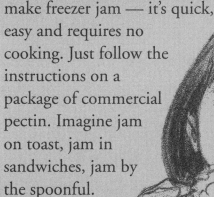

## GRANDMOTHER'S JAM

If the picking's plentiful, make jam with berries, apples and other fruits. See if your grandparent has a favorite family recipe. Or make freezer jam — it's quick, easy and requires no cooking. Just follow the instructions on a package of commercial pectin. Imagine jam on toast, jam in sandwiches, jam by the spoonful.

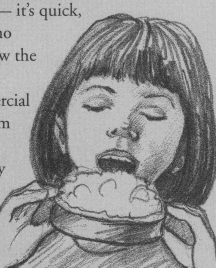

# PERFECT PICNIC

**N**owadays, an outdoor meal often means hamburgers and hot dogs from the barbecue. Here are some ideas for putting together an old-fashioned family picnic.

## GETTING READY

Prepare your meal indoors so it's ready to eat. Precut sandwiches and watermelon. Cover all food until you are ready to eat so you are less likely to get sand in your sandwich or attract ants and bees. Keep perishable food in the refrigerator or on ice until you are ready to eat so that it doesn't spoil. Plan a menu that uses little or no cutlery.

## CUCUMBER SANDWICHES

When your grandparents were kids, peanut butter may have been a rare treat. Kids back then ate cream cheese sandwiches with added layers of mint leaves and peeled, sliced raw cucumbers sprinkled with salt and pepper. Try one — they're crunchy and good. Or add a few slices of cucumber to your favorite peanut butter sandwich for an amazing mix of new and old.

## ANTS ON A LOG

Raw vegetables are always good to munch on. For a special treat, spread processed cheese inside a stalk of celery. Press a line of raisins into the cheese along the top to look like ants crawling on a log.

# DEVILED EGGS

Here's how to serve hard-boiled eggs so the yolk is creamy and doesn't stick to the roof of your mouth.

**YOU'LL NEED**

3 hard-boiled eggs, cooled

mayonnaise

mustard

salt and pepper

paprika

**1.** Crack the eggshells and peel them off the eggs.

**2.** Slice the eggs lengthwise and scoop out the yolk into the bowl.

**3.** Mash the yolks with the fork. Add 15 mL (1 tbsp.) mayonnaise and 2 mL (1/2 tsp.) mustard to the yolks and mash that in too.

**4.** Refill the cooked egg whites with the mashed yolk. Sprinkle with salt, pepper and paprika.

**5.** Cover with plastic wrap and chill until it is time to eat.

# OLD-FASHIONED LEMONADE

Prepare the syrup ahead of time. Then, add 30 mL (2 tbsp.) to every glass of chilled water (plain, soda or tonic water). Here's how to make the syrup:

**YOU'LL NEED**

500 mL (2 c.) sugar

250 mL (1 c.) water

the rind of 2 lemons cut into strips

a pinch of salt

juice of 6 lemons

**1.** Put the sugar, water and lemon rind in a pot on the stove and boil for five minutes.

**2.** Turn off the element. When the syrup is cool, add the juice from the lemons.

**3.** Store in a covered jar in the refrigerator until ready to mix.

# BREAKFAST IN BED

If you rise earlier in the morning than your grandparents, let them sleep in and treat them to breakfast in bed. Try these tasty no-cook recipes.

## BERRY GOOD ORANGE JUICE

The night before, place two large strawberries and one small glass in the freezer for each person you plan to serve. Don't forget to include yourself! In the morning, pour fresh orange juice into the frosty glasses and drop in the frozen berries. The berries will float on top and can be eaten when the juice is finished.

## SUNNY SOUTH FRUIT SALAD

Peel, slice and mix a colorful medley of fresh fruits together in a bowl. Good fruits to add include bananas, melons, oranges, berries, seedless grapes or other fruits your grandparents enjoy. If you have only a few fresh fruit slices, add a can of mandarin oranges or pineapple to the salad. If the mixture is dry, stir in several spoonfuls of apple, orange or pineapple juice.

## GRANOLA SUNDAE

### YOU'LL NEED

plain or vanilla yogurt

granola

fresh fruit such as peach slices or strawberries

honey or maple syrup (optional)

**1.** Spoon the yogurt into small bowls.

**2.** Sprinkle granola over the yogurt and top with a piece of fruit.

**3.** Dribble a spoonful of liquid honey or maple syrup over the top if you like it sweet.

# BAGEL AND CREAM CHEESE

**YOU'LL NEED**

15 mL (1 tbsp.) of chopped fresh parsley, dill, spring onion or other flavorful herbs (use 5 mL (1/4 tsp.) for dried herbs or onion)

50 mL ($1/4$ c.) cream cheese

a knife and spoon

a bagel

toaster

**1.** Stir the herbs or onion into the cream cheese.

**2.** Slice the bagel in two halves and toast to a golden brown.

**3.** Spread the toasted bagel with your flavored cream cheese. Serve with a sprig of whole parsley (or dill or onion) on the side of the plate.

## BREADS AND SPREADS

Toast is always a favorite, especially served with fresh jam. Sprinkle a little cinnamon and sugar on buttered toast for a sweet treat. For a change, toast English muffins and spread with marmalade.

# FAMILY FEAST

**H**ere's how you can get involved in preparing a family celebration. Wow your family with these creative table decorations. Everyone will feel welcome at your festive table.

## CHOCOLATE PLACE CARDS

Organize the seating with edible place cards. Once you've made the chocolate cards, decorate them with your own yummy icing.

**YOU'LL NEED**

500 mL (2 c.) chocolate chips

microwave-safe cup or double boiler

oven mitts

waxed paper

a cookie sheet

scissors

a spatula

a rolling pin

a ruler

a paring knife

**1.** Cover a cookie sheet with waxed paper. Trim with scissors.

**2.** Melt the chocolate on low heat, in the microwave or on the stove. Remove from the heat with oven mitts.

**3.** Pour the chocolate onto the prepared cookie sheet, spreading into the corners with a spatula.

**4.** Cover the chocolate with another piece of waxed paper. Gently roll with a rolling pin, until the chocolate is level.

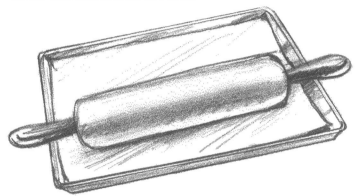

**5.** Place in the freezer for five minutes.

**6.** Remove the top piece of waxed paper. Using a ruler to guide the knife, cut the chocolate into 15 cm x 8 cm (6 in. x 3 in.) rectangles. If the chocolate is too brittle, wait a few minutes.

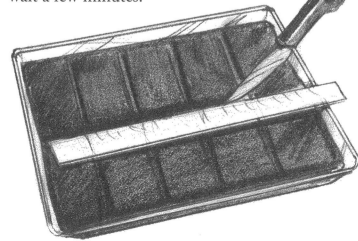

# ICING SCRIPT

**YOU'LL NEED**

1 egg white

5 mL (1 tsp.) lemon juice

500 mL (2 c.) icing sugar

a metal mixing bowl

an electric mixer or whisk

a spatula

a plastic 1-L (1 qt.) milk bag, washed and dried

scissors

**1.** In a metal mixing bowl, beat the egg white until frothy.

**2.** Add the lemon juice and beat again.

**3.** Add the sugar, 125 mL (¹/₂ c.) at a time, and continue beating until the icing is stiff, not runny. Add extra sugar if needed.

**4.** Scrape the icing into the plastic bag and push it to the bottom. Cut a tiny hole in one corner of the bag.

**5.** Practice icing writing on a piece of waxed paper. With one hand, hold the bag where the icing is and squeeze it out of the hole with the other.

**6.** Write a name on each chocolate place card. Decorate around the edges with a zigzag of icing.

# CRACKER FAVORS

These won't go pop like store-bought crackers, but you'll be able to personalize them for each guest.

**YOU'LL NEED**

slips of paper 2.5 cm x 8 cm (1 in. x 3 in.)

fine-tipped markers

a small favor (homemade or purchased) for each guest

cardboard toilet rolls

wrapping paper (recycled from other occasions)

ribbon

**1.** On slips of paper, write a greeting or fortune that suits each person.

**2.** Place a favor and the greeting inside a cardboard toilet roll.

**3.** Wrap the roll with wrapping paper, leaving space at each end. Tie the ends with small pieces of ribbon.

**4.** Using a marker, write each person's name on their cracker.

# DOUGH ORNAMENT CENTERPIECE

Baking dough can be molded or sculpted into many shapes. Braid the number 75 for your grandparent's birthday, make a family scene or fill a bowl with miniature pieces of fake fruit. Once baked and painted, your creations will be permanent art objects.

### YOU'LL NEED

250 mL (1 c.) salt
1 L (4 c.) flour
60 mL (2 oz.) glycerin
375 mL (1 1/2 c.) water
margarine
a large mixing bowl
waxed paper
a cookie sheet
tempera paints
a paintbrush
clear nail polish

**1.** Mix the salt and flour together in a large bowl.

**2.** Combine the glycerin and water and add to the salt and flour. Mix thoroughly, using your hands.

**3.** Knead, as one large ball of dough, for five minutes.

**4.** Divide into three or four balls the size of tennis balls and return to the bowl. Cover with waxed paper to keep moist.

**5.** Create a centerpiece to suit the occasion. Place all shaped dough on a lightly greased cookie sheet and bake at 150°C (300°F) for one hour, until light brown and hard. Large creations will take longer.

**6.** Remove from the oven with oven mitts and allow to cool. Paint as desired. When dry, add a coat of clear polish.

# CREATIVE CUTLERY

The cutlery drawer offers sculpting tools galore for your dough ornaments. Use a garlic press to form hair or a melon baller for the perfect circle. What can you do with cookie cutters, potato mashers, skewers, forks or apple corers?

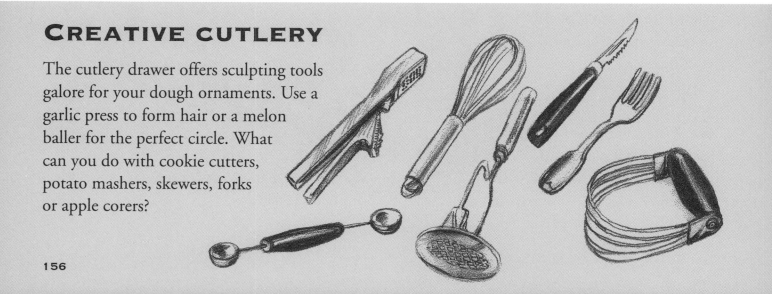

# NAPKIN FANS

Folded cloth napkins, held with a monogrammed napkin ring of ribbon, add a festive touch to your table

### YOU'LL NEED

cloth napkins

1 piece of cloth ribbon per person, 51 cm x 5 cm (20 in. x 2 in.)

a permanent marker

**1.** Write each family member's name on the middle of a piece of ribbon.

**2.** Fold the napkins up from the bottom to the middle and flatten with your hands. Starting at one side, fold the napkin, accordion style in 3 cm (1 1/4 in.) folds.

**3.** Hold in place with a ribbon, tying it so that the name appears on the top of the napkin. Place on the left side of each place setting.

## MIND YOUR MANNERS

What were the table rules when your grandparents were kids? They may have heard their parents say some of the following: "Children should be seen and not heard." "Sit up straight, with hands folded in your lap between bites." "Never put your elbows on the table." Find out more about dining codes of the past by digging into your grandparents' memories.

# INDEX

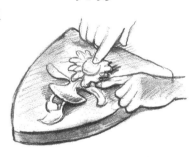

# ANSWERS

**Toothpick Teasers, page 54**

Puzzle 1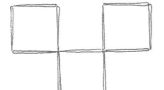

Puzzle 2

Puzzle 3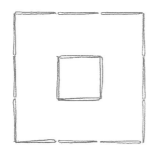

Puzzle 4

NINE

**Tangram pictures, page 57**

**Word Magic, page 64**

1. There were three fishermen: grandfather, father and son.

2. They are mother and son.

3. He's your father.